BATTLE IN AFRICA 1879-1914

HOWARD WHITEHOUSE

Illustrated by
Peter Dennis

Series Editor
Paddy Griffith

FIELD BOOKS

===== Contents =====

2 Africa before Partition
4 The Scramble for Africa
6 Strategic Concepts
8 Collecting an Army
10 Command
12 Collecting Supplies
14 Strategic Mobility
16 Reconnaissance and Signals
18 March Security
20 The African Response
22 Closing with the Enemy
24 Tamai

26 European Battle Plans
28 African Battle Plans
30 African Leadership
32 The New Technology
34 The Power of Fire
36 Cold Steel
38 Horrible Disasters
40 Glorious Victories
42 Guerrilla Warfare
44 Siege Warfare
46 After the Battle

Published by Fieldbooks, 47 Owlsmoor Road, Camberley, Surrey GU15 4SW

© Copyright 1987 Fieldbooks. All rights reserved. ISBN 1 869871 01 4

Africa before Partition

Europeans in the 1870s were starting to find out about, and become fascinated by, Africa. A mass market was opening for cheap, popular literature: tales of savage barbarism and clean-limbed heroism. 'Africans' danced in the music halls; speculators dreamed of fortunes to be made; clergymen of souls to be saved. Livingstone and Stanley became figureheads of a new brand of aggressive philanthropy, and Africa became an El Dorado where the ambitions of a whole generation of Europeans - to do good or to do well - could be pursued.

Samuel and Florence Baker visit an African village.

European traders in Africa were no novelty. The coastal cities of North Africa had been an integral part of the 'Mediterranean Civilisation' for thousands of years. European 'Voyages of Discovery' from Vasco da Gama (late 15th century) onwards had brought meetings, understandings and trade. A complex network of trade grew up between European slavers and their African middlemen until the suppression of the slave trade in 1807, when a changeover to other forms of commerce took place. Palm oil, rubber, ivory, gold dust, cotton and coffee replaced the traffic in human chattels - although slaving vessels continued to make the 'Middle Passage' to Cuba and Brazil until the 1880s. All these transactions were still based on equality between African and European - but this was soon to change.

European missionaries came to Africa with the traders. First the Jesuits in Angola and Mozambique in the 16th century, then the other organised Christian mission groups elsewhere from the start of the 19th century. Anglican and Methodist missions emerged in Sierra Leone and their educated converts - Africans rescued from the slave ships - spread throughout the coastal zone of West Africa. Presbyterians came to the Gold Coast in the 1820s, and by the 1850s every major Christian denomination had missions on the 'Guinea Coast'. Often ignorant and intolerant of the traditional values of their self-selected charges, these missionaries nevertheless maintained a firm humanitarian spirit: John Philip of the London Missionary society was outspoken against the Cape Boers, while in Madagascar the society taught 4,000 Hova to read and write their own language between 1820 and 1827. Most celebrated was David Livingstone, whose journeys (1853-73) inspired Victorians to come to the 'Dark Continent' for worldly reasons as well as to spread the word of the Lord.

European explorers enjoyed their golden age in the 19th century. Mungo Park, Rêné Caillié and Heinrich Barth visited the Niger region before 1850; later adventurers included Sir Richard Burton, Samuel Baker, J H Speke and dozens more. Their narratives of colourful and exotic lands drew an enormous popular interest until in the 1870s their influence - often motivated more by reputation than by science - weighed heavily with the governments of Europe. H M Stanley, the Welsh-American journalist who 'found' Livingstone in 1871, was employed by the Belgian King Leopold to explore the Congo for its commercial prospects (1875-85). During the same period Count Pierre Savorgnan de Brazza was surveying equatorial Africa for the French. Karl Peters of the Society for German Colonisation provided his government with its ticket to a slice of East Africa by his 'treaties' of 1884-5.

THE MAGHRIB of North West Africa was particularly vulnerable to the European advance. **Algiers** fell to the French in 1830 and years of 'pacification' followed. 100,000 soldiers protected the influx of white colonists who took the best land, yet Kabylia remained unsubdued and constant military operations were still required.

Morocco was defeated by France in 1845 and by Spain in 1895-60. The Sultan found it difficult to control his nomadic subjects and the Marabouts (religious leaders). Yet Moulai al-Hasan, Sultan from 1873, asserted his authority by strong military action, and did much to avoid provocative frontier incidents against the Europeans.

Tunisia was ruled by a Regency under Turkish suzerainty, and its reforms - including the abolition of slavery - made a model for the Maghrib. Yet the Bey was unable to control his western hill tribes, and their incursions into Algeria were to provide an excuse for the furtherance of French ambitions in the area.

WEST AFRICA consisted of the grassland belt of Western Sudan in the north, and a forest zone to the southwest.

In the **Western Sudan** - long the home of great empires - the Fulani empire established by Uthman Dan Fodio held Hausaland (modern northern Nigeria) as far east as Kanem-Bornu and south into the old Oyo empire of the Yorubas. The Tukolor empire of Al-Hajj Umar (died 1864) lay to the west, now under his son Ahmadu Sefu, while in the southwest the Mandinka soldier Samori Touré created a major state in the 1870s.

The **Forest Zone** was controlled by centralised nations - Dahomey, Asante (Ashanti), Benin and Yoruba states, as well as several less formally governed tribal groups. The Asante were a military confederation who dominated the coastal Fanti, although repeated clashes with British traders had brought Sir Garnet Wolseley's expedition, 1873-4, which captured their capital.

French Senegal was the most significant of the European coastal trading enclaves. Louis Faidherbe, the governor from 1854, had extended his possessions through Futa Toro into conflict with Al Hajj Umar: the first of many similar clashes.

In 1821 the Afro-American settlement of **Liberia** had been established, and it has maintained its independence of the Europeans to this day.

Battle in Africa

NORTH EAST AFRICA
In **Egypt** ambitious modernisation plans based on the Suez canal brought bankruptcy, and control by an international debt commission. This in turn produced discontent and a military rebellion. The Khedive Ismail was deposed in 1879 but his successor - his son Tawfiq - fell into the power of the radical army officer Arabi Pasha.

The Sudan had been conquered by Egypt in the 1820s and Khedive Ismail had pushed his military expansion still further, extending down the Red Sea and on to Kismayu (1865-75). Corruption and religious grievances, however, provoked a rebellion against the Egyptians. Muhammad Ahmad, the self-proclaimed Mahdi ('Saviour'), led the Sudanese in a series of victories (1881-85).

In the isolated Christian empire of **Ethiopia**, the British had intervened in 1868 to defeat the Emperor Theodoros (Tewodoros) and eventually had him replaced by John (Johannis). John overcame domestic anarchy, weathered the Egyptian expansion down the Red Sea, and by 1880 he was poised to expand against the Moslems and pagans to south and east - but his own throne was threatened by a young rival, Menelik of Shoa.

In **Tripoli** the Turks had re-asserted their authority in 1835, although in the interior of Cyrenaica the Bedouin rallied to the Sanusi - a fundamentalist Moslem brotherhood. Sanusi influence spread across the Sahara to Bornu and Wadai, and much of the desert trade fell into their hands.

EAST AFRICA was dominated by the Swahili-Arab Trading Empire, loosely subject to the Sultan of Zanzibar. Their raids into the interior, in search of slaves and ivory, shocked both Livingstone and his Victorian readers but brought an hegemony extending as far as the Great Lakes and the Eastern Congo basin. A Nyamwezi trader, Mirambo, built a kingdom east of Lake Tanganyika in the 1870s when he found himself pushed back by the better-organised coastmen.

The **East African Plain** was inhabited by pastoral peoples such as the Somali or the fierce Maasai, or by farmers such as the Hehe.

Populous centralised states such as Buganda, Bunyoro and Ankhole had been established on the fertile lands of the lake region, isolated until they were reached by Arab traders in 1844. They fascinated the explorers Burton, Baker and Speke, and in 1874-6 recieved envoys from General Gordon.
The Zanzibar Sultanate exercised only an informal authority, although its Arab cities were effectively ruled by Seyyid Said (1806-56), and there was a secure credit system and a guaranteed market for trade.

EQUATORIAL AFRICA The River Congo and its great belt of rain forest had fascinated Europeans since the early Portuguese voyages. In the 19th century Portugal still held small, neglected coastal enclaves in Angola and Cabinda. Inland lay centralised African states. The Luba and Lunda in the west were being displaced by the well-armed Chokwe ivory hunters, and in the east by the Nyamwezi and the Arabs. In Katanga the trader Msiri established a military-mercantile kingdom between 1856 and 1891. By 1860 the Arabs had settled on the Lualaba, destroying existing kingdoms, and by 1870 their paramount leader Tippu Tib, had carved out an enormous kingdom in the Eastern Congo. With allegedly 50,000 guns at his command, he nevertheless remained faithful to the distant Sultan of Zanzibar.

Also in the rain forest region were several smaller peoples - Bobangi, Teke and the ferocious - reputedly Cannibal - Fang.

A jubilant Zulu with captured rifle and equipment after Isandhlwana, 1879.

SOUTHERN AFRICA was inhabited by many disparate peoples. The oldest were the Khoisan 'Hottentots' of the Western Cape who interbred with Europeans, and primitive 'Bushmen' groups who were driven remorselessly into the Kalahari. Then in the early 19th century came a serious population explosion among the Southern Bantu, as they came into contact with the Boers. By 1879 the chief Bantu peoples were the Xhosa, Pondo, Gaekas and Gcalekas (who were beaten by the British 1877-8), the Sotho, Swazis - and the Zulu empire. In the far west were the Bechuanas and Herero, while driven north of the Limpopo by the Boers were the Ndebele (Matabele) and their subjects the Shona and Barotse.

On the high veldt were two Africaner republics. Descendents of Dutch settlers, the Boers were independent, individualist and convinced of their God-given racial superiority. Following the British takeover of the Cape in 1815, they had trekked north and defeated the Zulus (1839-40) and Ndebele (1837), but in 1877 the British proclaimed the annexation of both the Transvaal and the Orange Free State.

Madagascar was dominated by the sophisticated Merina state of the Hovas, but French influence was strong and they controlled most of the commerce.

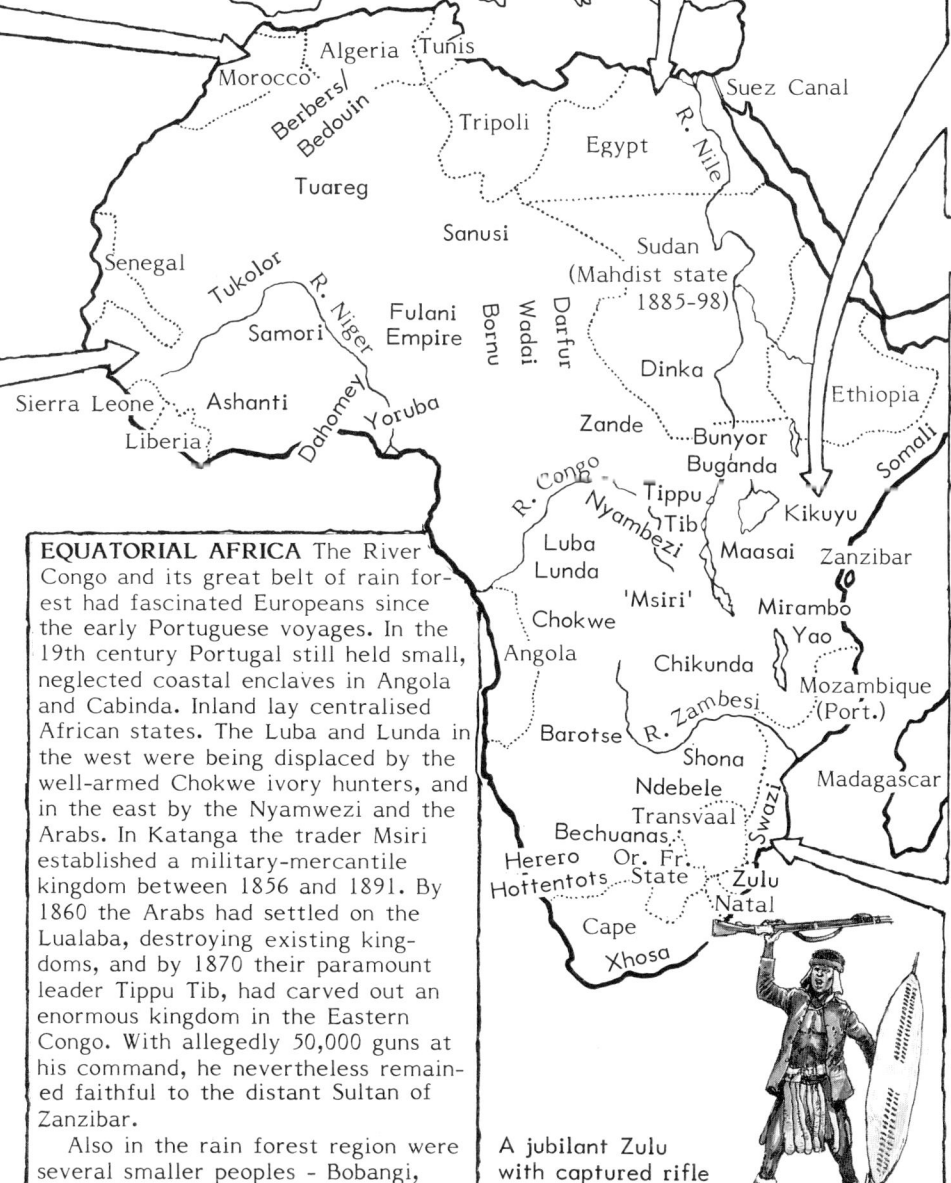

The Scramble for Africa

Between 1879 and 1914 the Europeans carved up Africa. The reasons for this were many - hope of economic gains, belief in the 'Civilising Mission', strategic advantage, the pressure of excess populations and, most of all, prestige. The French sought to make up for the humiliation of 1870; the Italians to prove themselves a 'power'; the British and Portuguese to maintain their early lead. The establishment of King Leopold's 'Congo Free State' after the Brussels Conference of 1876 began the scramble - then the conquest of Tunis and Egypt advanced it, and the Berlin Conference (1884-5) confirmed it. A complex series of treaties divided Africa, without reference to the wishes of Africans. Meanwhile the doctrines of 'Spheres of Influence' and 'Effective Occupation' dictated that the race on the ground started in earnest. Despite some serious quarrels (eg Fashoda 1898 between France and Britain, or Agadir 1911 between Germany and France) the Europeans stood together in observing their drawing-room accords. The result was a sudden, unanimous spate of conquests throughout Africa which left only Liberia and Ethiopia free from European control by 1914.

Africa in 1914

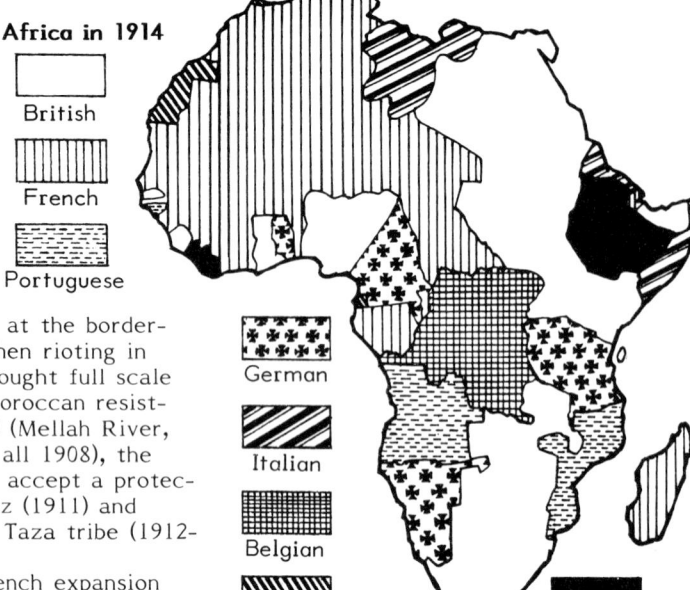

British
French
Portuguese
German
Italian
Belgian
Spanish
Independent

THE FRENCH EMPIRE

The Maghrib By 1879 the French had consolidated a position in Algeria and were making plans for expansion. Incursions by Krumir tribesmen from Tunisia provided an excuse for the annexation of Tunis (May 1881), then a second expedition defeated the mountain tribes - capturing Kayruwan before the year's end. The advance into the Sahara also pushed ahead - to Touggourt 1882, El Golea 1887, In Salah 1900. The Tuareg wiped out the Flatters railway survey mission in 1880-1, but the steel rails still followed French columns, confirming possession. In South Oranais the Sheriff Bou Amana raised a Jihad in 1882; inflicted a serious loss on a Foreign Legion column at Chott Tigri (1882), and proved such a nuisance to the French that they eventually gave him a pension! At El Moungar in 1902 a supply column was ambushed and mauled by Shaamba Arabs, and in the same year the Ahaggar Tuareg were defeated at Tit. In 1905 the Trarza and Brakna Moors in Mauretania attacked the expedition of the French agent Coppolani at Tdjikdja, and killed him.

In Morocco the Sultan's efforts to maintain his independence by exploiting European divisions finally broke down. Under General Lyautey the French chewed away at the borderlands (1903-7), and then rioting in Casablanca (1907) brought full scale invasion. Although Moroccan resistance was determined (Mellah River, M'Karto, Menablia - all 1908), the Sultan was forced to accept a protectorate. Risings at Fez (1911) and among the Tache de Taza tribe (1912-14) were suppressed.

West Africa The French expansion eastward along the Senegal-Niger river system brought a series of military conquests. The Damel of Cayor was defeated and killed in 1886, and the Soninka peoples led by Mamadou Lamine were defeated at Touba-Kouta in1887. Ahmadu Sefu had aided the French against Mamadou but then himself fell victim to them, losing actions at Koundian (1889), Segu (1890) and Youri (1891), and finally fleeing to Sokoto. Samori Touré made a brilliant resistance (1882-98) by diplomacy, effective strategy, and even by moving his entire empire 400 miles to the east. Yet he too was eventually captured and exiled. Timbuktu fell in 1894 when Joffre avenged the destruction of the 1893 Bonnier column at the hands of the Tuareg. By 1900 columns from Algeria, Central Africa and the Western Sudan met at Lake Chad to conquer Rabih at the Battle of Kousseri.

The French also took Dahomey (1892-4), but found great difficulties against the Baule of the Ivory Coast, who resisted from 1891 to 1911. Meanwhile the French expanded their Gabon base - probing north east into Ubangi-Shari as far as Lake Chad by 1900. They also engaged in the conquest of Madagascar following the indecisive war of 1883-5. Fever and rough terrain delayed Duchesne's invasion of 1895, but a flying column beat the Hovas at Tsynainondry and took their capital. The rising of the 'Red Plaids' in 1896 was suppressed, and Gallieni undertook the military unification of the island (1897-1904). The leading French colonial officer of his day, he was nevertheless unable to prevent frequent local risings against European rule.

Germany's 'Place in the Sun' was widely scattered across Africa, as the Germans entered the colonial race rather late and were left to pick up territories which no one else had bothered to seize. These included Togo and the Cameroons (1884) - whence the eastern Fulani cities were later annexed. Further south the Germans founded a colony in South West Africa (1884), where there was fighting against Hendrick Witbooi's Hottentots (1892-4). In 1904 the Herrero rose to regain their land and cattle, and inflicted major defeats on the Europeans before being savagely put down. Just as the Hereros were suppressed, the Hottentots rose again under Hendrick and the brilliant Morenga (1904-7). In East Africa Germany secured the Sultan of Zanzibar's territory in Tanganyika. The 'Arab Rebellion' of Abushiri was defeated (1888-9) and the long resistance of the Wahehe was overcome (1891-8). German rule was harsh and exploitative in the extreme, provoking the Maji-Maji rising of 1905-7. This was a collective action of the southern peoples united by religious leaders. It was heavily suppressed, after confidence that ancestors would return to defeat the invader proved to be unfounded.

Battle in Africa

THE BRITISH EMPIRE

North East Africa The revolutionary government of Arabi Pasha threatened European investments in Egypt, so after a bombardment of Alexandria in 1882 a British expedition under Wolseley was despatched. In a brilliant campaign he feinted towards Aboukir then seized the Suez Canal and stormed the entrenchments of Tel El Kebir, covering Cairo. His ferocious pursuit secured him the whole of Egypt which was to remain under British control until 1922.

In the Sudan, however, the Mahdist rebellion was rapidly gaining strength. Egyptian authority had collapsed after the massacre of Hicks Pasha's army and the fall of El Obeid (1883) leaving only a few besieged garrisons. Osman Digna won those on the Red Sea for the Mahdi, but was defeated twice by the British in 1884 - at El Teb and Tamai. General Gordon, in Khartoum could not hold out and was killed. The relief expedition beat the Mahdists at Abu Klea and Abu Kru in 1885, but was too late to save him. After another Red Sea expedition, the Sudan was abandoned by the British to the Mahdi's successor, the Khalifa. He repeatedly overcame internal revolts, but disastrously failed to invade Egypt in 1889. The Egyptian reconquest of the Sudan got under way at Firket in 1896 and ended at Omdurman two years later. The Khalifa was killed in 1899; a Mahdist revival was suppressed in 1908, and the Dinka and Nuer peoples were subdued.

East Africa By 1890 Zanzibar was a British protectorate - a fact confirmed by a few minutes of naval gunfire in 1896. In Uganda, British control came when Lugard's Maxim gun won the battle of Mengo in 1892 on behalf of the Ganda protestants. The victors went on to overthrow their ruler Mwanga, and Kabarega of Bunyoro, in 1899. A mutiny of the Sudanese soldiery was put down in 1897, and the Uganda railway was completed in 1901. Meanwhile Kenya was being conquered by a series of wars against the Mazrui family of Mombassa, the Akamba, Kisii and Kikuyu. The Nandi submitted only in 1906 - after six expeditions against them - when the British suppressed the tribe with great brutality.

West Africa British expansion from their coastal enclaves gave them control over the Nigerian trading states (Ijebu in 1892, Oyo in 1895), the empire of Benin (1897), the Tiv and the Ibo peoples. The oracle of the Aro Ibo was destroyed in 1901. Campaigns against Bida and Ilorin (1897), Kano and Sokoto (1903), broke the Fulani emirate of northern Nigeria. Asante was conquered in two campaigns (1896, 1900), the Temne and Mende of Sierra Leone were suppressed in the Hut Tax War (1898), and the Gambia territory was secured by the defeat of Marabout leaders Fode Silla (1894) and Fode Kabba (1900).

Southern Africa The British invasion of Zululand (1879) was halted by the disaster of Isandhlwana, but the defence of Rorke' Drift and the continued presence of columns at Eshowe and Kambula kept the campaign alive until reinforcements arrived to defeat the Zulu king Cetshwayo at Ulundi. Later in the year the resistance of the Sekukini and the Pedi was crushed. In 1880 the Transvaal Boers rose against British rule: in four battles the British were beaten, and after the death of General Colley in the debacle of Majuba Hill (1881), the Boer republics gained their independence. In 1890 Cecil Rhodes' British South Africa Company occupied Mashonaland: war with the Ndebele came in 1893 and, despite a victory over the Shangane Patrol, Lobengula was beaten and died in flight. In 1896 the Ndebele and Shona rose against settler oppression in the Chimurenga they were put down with great bloodshed the following year, although resistance continued until 1903.

The Second Boer War (1899-1902) began with a series of British defeats, culminating in the disastrous 'Black Week' of three lost battles (Magersfontein, Stormberg and Colenso) in December 1899. The arrival of Lord Roberts secured the Boer capitals in 1900, but an effective guerilla war continued for another two years. Later, there was an African rising in Natal (1906) and a minor Boer revolt in favour of the Germans in 1914.

Portuguese attempts to take 'effective occupation' of Angola led to the campaigns of Artur de Piava in the Cubango region (1885-8), and a series of risings, of which the Bailundo War (1902) is the best remembered. Not until 1915, when 7,000 metropolitan troops were sent against the Cuanhama, did Portugal have real authority over all Angola. In Mozambique the Portuguese drive inland met repeated defeats at the hands of the Chikunda in the Zambezi valley, but more success in the coastal region where Gungunyane's rising (which had captured Lourenco Marques in 1894) was put down by the end of 1896.

The Congo Free State was King Leopold's private venture - a coastal station which gradually expanded up-river. An alliance with Tippu Tib broke down into open war (1891-4) which the Free-Staters won by superior organisation and weaponry - capturing Nyangwe in 1893 and Ujiji in 1894. In 1890 the Belgian advance also reached the Congo-Nile divide, established a foothold at Lado on the Nile and defeated the Mahdists at Rejaf and Bedden (1897-8). In Katanga Msiri was shot dead during 'negotiations' and his kingdom annexed.

Leopold's administration was astonishingly brutal, provoking desperate resistance - a 20 year war with the Chokwe; rebellions by Budja and Bowa tribesmen forced into rubber plantations, and in 1897 a serious mutiny in the 'Force Publique' itself. Altogether some five million Congolese died under Leopold's rule.

The Italians seized Eritrea (1882-90), whence they entered Ethiopia, then ruled by the Emperor John. An Italian force was massacred at Dogali in 1887, but John died fighting the Mahdists two years later at Gallabat. He was succeeded by Menelik, who had good relations with Italy and preferred to march against the Galla and Somali tribes to the south. However by 1895 he too was at war with the Italians, and beat them at Amba Alagi and then Adowa (1896) - a decisive victory which guaranteed Ethiopian independence for forty years. In 1897 the Italians also had to face - alongside the British in the Horn of Africa - the Somali Jihad of Al-Sayyid Muhammed. This war continued until 1920 and the Somalis won several victories, including Gamburu Hill (1903) and Dul Madoba (1913).

In 1911 the Italians invaded the Ottoman provinces of Tripoli and Cyrenaica. Despite success in the battles of Al Hani, Al Hawwari (1911), Al Nadura and Al Mudawwar (1912), the Turks were forced to withdraw by the European powers. Resistance nevertheless continued, led by the Sanusi, and the invaders were badly beaten at Yawm Al-Djuma (1913). In the following year Italian strength and organisation prevailed at Djanduba and Sabha, and at least a measure of control over the area was achieved.

Strategic Concepts

Campaigns were planned either for conquest or for punishment. When the intention was occupation, force was allied to political initiatives and schemes for 'pacification'. When the object was simply to 'discipline' a recalcitrant people, a policy of despoilation was often preferred - the torch was cheaper than the sword. The French 'Razzia' especially raised desolation into a fine art - but the theft or killing of herds, destruction of orchards and use of rapacious irregulars (and regulars too!) for reprisal pillaging were methods common to all the European powers.

Some aims of European campaigns were:

A To relieve a besieged outpost - a limited objective which could none the less involve huge forces, eg Buller's 1899 campaign to relieve Ladysmith.

B To capture the enemy's capital. The three Asante campaigns were all directed towards Kumasi, the French invasion of Madagascar towards Tananarive.

C To defeat the enemy army. Although Chelmsford's 1879 campaign was aimed at the Zulu capital, Ulundi. the essential object was to destroy the Zulu army threatening Natal.

D To take the enemy's leaders, or other symbols of sovereignty - eg the Asante 'Golden Stool'. The French war against Samori was ended by his capture; and pursuit of Ceteshwayo, Lobengula and Behanzin of Dahomey was deemed necessary for genuine victory in each case.

The French School Whereas the soldiers of the Queen were subordinate to civilian masters within each colony, the French empire in Africa was largely the consequence of decisions made entirely by military men. Thus 'The French School' emphasised the role of the soldier as administrator, and of strategy as part of an overall policy of 'pacific occupation'. In the 1840s Marshal Bugeaud had proposed a strategy of mobile light columns for Algeria, supported by the settlement of veterans in military villages. Fifty years later Gallieni advanced a theory of colonial warfare, based on his experiences in Senegal and Western Sudan, which called for his pupils - among them the future Marshals Joffre and Lyautey - to throw away their textbooks and rely on experience. In Tonkin (1891-6) and then in Madagascar, Gallieni's 'pacifications' were based on a firm military blow followed immediately by the creation of markets, schools and clinics for the beaten foe - all under the authority of the 'cercles militaires' (military administrators). This system was popularised by Lyautey in his article on the 'Role Coloniale de l'Armee' (1900). Lyautey proposed what he called the 'oil-stain' approach, whereby French 'zones of influence' would grow by attracting tribesmen to markets and amenities rather than by simply sending punitive columns or establishing outposts. As an 'organisation on the march', peaceful occupation was to accompany, rather than to follow, the Army of Africa.

Lyautey's warfare therefore used broad fronts rather than supporting columns, but it retained Bugeaud's belief in boldness, planning and mobility - 'In Africa one defends oneself by moving'. The principles of siegecraft were also applied to mountain fighting - encircling centres of opposition by pincer movements, pulling the noose tight, then assaulting the starving and demoralised enemy. Lyautey's ideas were not always as effective as he claimed, however, since in South Oranais and Morocco (1903-25) he said much about 'native politics' and working with local authorities, but actually still relied heavily upon the Razzia and straightforward firepower.

Legionnaires with prisoners.

Menelik, Emperor of Ethiopia, gives an audience to an Italian Emissary.

Politics. The role of any commander always had a political dimension. He had to follow, interpret or disregard the directives of distant ministers who had little idea of 'events on the ground'. Orders from Rome demanding 'Any sacrifice to save the honour of the army and the prestige of the monarchy' led directly to the Italian catastrophe of Adowa. On a local level, equally, commanders had to devise and implement their own policies. Alliances with tribal leaders could bring warriors, scouts and supplies - and a useful element of 'divide and rule' for the future. Frederick Lugard even admitted that many of his treaties were fraudulent - but he made them anyway, and became a successful exponent of Imperial policy in both East Africa and Nigeria. Sometimes, however, treaties could backfire - eg the Witbois Hottentots used guns and know-how they had obtained from the Germans in their insurrection against the Germans themselves.

Battle in Africa

Callwell and the British School Major C E Callwell, a British artilleryman, wrote his classic 'Small Wars, Their Principles and Practice' in 1896. He recognised that the accepted theories of continental warfare had but little relevance to imperial campaigning, so he put forward his own clear and insightful thesis to fill the gap. His message, based on analysis of a broad array of colonial campaigns, was that successful strategy depended less upon complex maneouvre than on sound logistics and boldness of purpose. The conduct of small wars, wrote Callwell, was 'an art by itself'.

He emphasised that resolution was essential to success, holding 'that the initiative must be maintained, that the regular army must lead while its adversaries follow, and that the enemy must be made to feel a moral inferiority throughout.' A vigorous offensive strategy was the key, seeking out the enemy and forcing decisive battle upon him whenever and wherever he might be found. Delays could prove disastrous, and would certainly encourage the enemy. Callwell therefore held that it was better to postpone the start of a campaign until the forces were fully organised, equipped and ready. 'Organisation' included careful consideration of supply and transport, the use of information, and the study of the theatre of operations. In some circumstances 'flying columns' carrying all their own provisions would be employed - but at other times a lengthy line of communication was better. Aggressive strategy founded on firm logistics and intelligence would, Callwell claimed, lead to success.

Anatomy of a campaign Organising a campaign in a distant and inaccessible land was always an impressive feat, but when haste was obligatory, it could prove a nightmare. The Gordon Relief Expedition was authorised on 8th August 1884; Sir Garnet Wolseley was given command on the 26th, and by September 9th he was in Cairo. Pausing until the 27th to organise troops, stores and boats, he reached Assuan by private yacht on 1st October, Wadi Halfa on the 5th, and thence to Dongola and Korti. But the mobilisation of supplies and soldiers was far slower - eg the Guards Camel Regiment left London on 26th September, reached Halfa on 12th November and, after training at Dongola, arrived at Korti on 14th December. The boat-borne infantry was still slower - the best speed from Sarras to Korti was 38 days - less than 9 miles per day on average. Elaborate staffwork was needed to tie the complex transport plans together. On 28th January 1885 the spearhead of the army reached Khartoum - too late to save Gordon, but remarkably early by the normal standards of the day. Despite confusion, squabbling and errors, the campaign was an astonishing example of successful improvisation. Kitchener's careful reconquest a decade later was to take two years - ie almost five times as long as Wolseley's campaign.

The Gordon Relief Expedition 1884-5

1 London-Cairo The Voyage by steamer took 10-15 days to Alexandria, followed by a rail journey of 120 miles to British HQ in Cairo. From here there was a telegraph link to London and - until it was cut - Khartoum.

2 Cairo-Assiut The Egyptian rail system covered the distance of around 200 miles to Assiut, and later Balliana.

3 Assiut-Assuan Tourist steamers belonging to Thomas Cook & Co., together with a variety of tugs, barges and local river craft, transported troops on this 300 mile reach of the Nile. The Gordon Relief Expedition was delayed for three weeks when Cooks ran out of coal.

4 Assuan-Shellal The 7 miles of rocks and rapids making up the First Cataract were by-passed by a narrow-gauge railway.

5 Shellal-Wadi Halfa A second flotilla of steamers and Nile boats ('Nuggurs' and 'Gyasas') sailed this 215 mile leg

6 Wadi Halfa-Sarras A narrow-gauge railway circumvented the Second Cataract and ran on 33 miles to Sarras. For the 1896 invasion of Dongola the line was extended another 75 miles to Kosheh.

7 Sarras-Korti 330 miles, including 22 miles of white water between the Second and Third Cataracts. Korti was the advanced base for the Relief Expedition - the telegraph and lines of communication to Cairo ended here. Beyond this point only flying columns, advancing 'into the blue', could operate.

8A Korti-Mettemma The 176 miles of caravan route across the Bayuda desert was broken at the wells of Jakdul (90 miles) and Abu Klea (153 miles). Rather than make the eight-day journey in one stage, Stewart's desert column established a forward supply depot at Jakdul wells. This meant much stronger logistical support for the column, but involved more than doubling the journey time to 22 days in all.

8B Korti-Berber The bulk of the force continued by whale boat the 270 miles to Berber, averaging only 4 miles per day. While it took 31 days to reach the Nile column's furthest point, 30 miles short of Abu Hamed, it came back in 9!

9 Mettemma-Khartoum The final leg was 76 miles, with a party of soldiers, dressed in red coats to impress the locals, transported in two of the remaining steamers. Delayed on starting they took four tortuous days to ascend the falling river - and found the Mahdists had captured the city two days before.

Collecting an Army

To engage in colonial warfare, a European power needed an army. Since African campaigns were expensive, and frequently unpopular, there was a strong preference for keeping this army small - making for the cheapest possible 'effective use of force.'

MOBILISATION SEQUENCE: How colonial authorities might provide troops -

1 Local Garrisons and other troops 'on the spot' might be few in number, if the war was a consequence of an African initiative. Europeans were often taken by surprise, eg at the start of Abushiri's revolt the German 'Defence Force' in East Africa comprised 600 Sudanese, 50 Somalis and 350 Zulus - a diverse collection of men, vastly outnumbered by the Swahili rebels. Even when local forces were large - such as the 14,750 regular British troops in South Africa in 1899 - they might be inadequate to deal with the threat.

2 New recruits and alliances would rapidly be sought. Hastily-formed units would be drilled and organised, while the 'enemies of the enemy' would be approached and offered loot, privileges and a chance to settle old scores. The British force that defeated the Sekukuni was mainly made up of their traditional foes the Swazis.

3 Nearby possessions of the same European nation might be asked to help, if local resources were inadequate, eg the French in Morocco could call on Algeria; the British in the 1896 Asante campaign employed Hausa infantry from Nigeria. In the wake of the disaster at Isandhlwana, the garrison of peaceful St Helena was rushed to Natal. 'Naval Brigades' from warships might also be formed.

4 An expedition from Europe would be despatched if the war was considered a really serious matter - often this meant a 'black mark' against the men on the spot who had apparently failed to cope with the crisis. The British government frequently sent units from India to help in its African wars - they were geographically close, experienced in small wars, and free from the unwelcome scrutiny of the opposition in parliament.

5 Reinforcements were sent only when the war was going very badly - when a home government was forced to ward off a potential blow to its prestige. Buller failed to beat the Boers with 47,000 men, so thousands more were sent - bringing numbers up to 180,000 in February 1900. The Germans eventually deployed 20,000 regulars to defeat 8,000 Herero warriors (many unarmed), and then 1,500 Hottentots, taking four years to do it.

Sir Garnet Wolseley speaks to the Colonel of a newly-arrived regiment. Alexandria, 1882

Appointing a commander. Between 1871 and 1914 the European officer caste was eager to see action wherever it could be found. There was great competition to get an appointment, preferably a good one, in any expeditionary force bound for Africa. In general the command would be given to the man on the spot, as long as he had the proper rank and seniority. But if he did not resolve matters quickly, he was likely to be replaced. Thus the experienced Von Leutwein was succeeded first by Von Trotha and then by Von Deimling, as the Germans sought to reverse their humiliating series of disasters in South West Africa. Equally Lord Chelmsford was anxious to beat the Zulus once and for all before his replacement, Wolseley, arrived. The latter reciprocated by making strenuous efforts to reach the field army in time to win the glory for himself. Wolseley was ambitious, and would pressure political leaders to appoints him to the command of each and every large British expedition - then he would select his own staff from a favoured group of experienced officers known as the 'Ashanti Ring' (from their service in the 1873-4 campaign). Naturally this procedure caused friction with those outside the clique - eg supporters of the arch-conservative Duke of Cambridge, and later the 'Indians' who looked to Lord Roberts for leadership. In France the officers of the metropolitan army looked down on the 'Troupes de Marine' and 'Armee d'Afrique' who were not 'smart' and whose leaders - Bazaine, Canrobert and MacMahon - had been responsible for the 1870 defeats. Such conflicts frequently meant that plum jobs went not to those who most deserved them, but to those who were best placed to pull strings.

Training and acclimatisation was essential for newly-arrived troops, who had to respond to unfamiliar conditions. Old hands would try to disabuse officers of the notion that African campaigning was a kind of glorified big game hunt. Soldiers were 'trained' to ride camels or ponies in what Kipling called 'Three days to learn equitation an' six months o' bloomin' well trot'. Men needed time to adjust to the climate; the crack Rifle Brigade and Grenadier Guards - fresh from the Mediterranean in 1898 - compared badly with units that had been longer in the Sudan, and suffered terribly from sunstroke. Animals also needed to regain 'condition'. When forced to march for endless miles on strange fodder immediately after a long sea voyage, mules and horses died off quickly.

Battle in Africa

British infantry 1879 | *British Camel Corps 1884* | *Italian Bersaglieri 1894* | *Bombay infantry, Sudan 1885* | *Senegalese Spahis (French) 1889* | *French 'Turco' 1889* | *Maasai warrior*

European regulars were usually prestigious soldiers: expert in drill and well equipped. However, they were often inexperienced in anything more than 'square-bashing'. Smart Guards or Heavy Cavalry units were imposing and supremely confident - but were far less flexible or skilled in fieldcraft than lowly County regiments which had seen more active service.

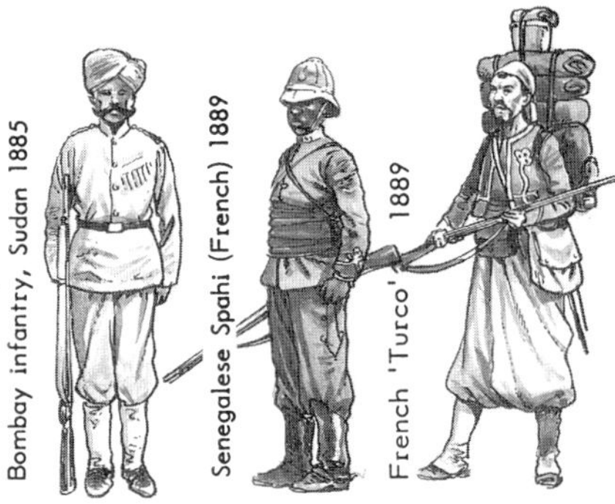

Regulars recruited for colonial service could be highly efficient if they were well trained. The French 'Armée d'Afrique' featured Spahis, Turcos, Chasseurs d'Afrique, Zouaves and the legendary Foreign Legion. British India provided Sikhs, Gurkhas, Punjab regiments and Bengal Lancers.
The field companies of German South West Africa were effective and mobile - the Hereos called them 'men' whereas they termed green troops from Germany 'boys'.

Local tribes were often more than willing to help the Europeans against their traditional enemies. The British used Maasai to fight the Nandi, and the Ganda to invade Bunyoro. The Beni Amir supported Italy against Abyssinia, while Ahmadu Sefu allied with the French (when he was not fighting against them). Karl Peters made a classic appeal to a Nyanwezi caravan: 'Come and help us. If we capture the herds of the Wagogo you shall have a share in the booty.'

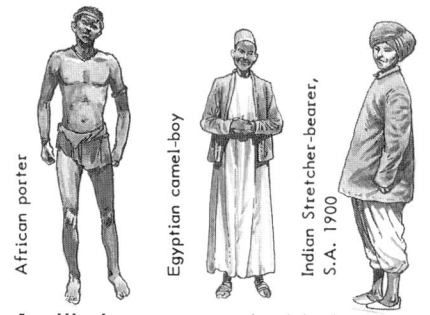

Natal Native Horse 1879 | *Imperial Yeomanry Scout 1901* | *Boer volunteer 1880* | *Frontier Light Horse 1879* | *African porter* | *Egyptian camel-boy* | *Indian Stretcher-bearer, S.A. 1900*

Locally-raised troops varied from poor - eg the Natal Native Contingent - to very good - eg Goldie's Hausa constabulary; the Tirailleurs Sénégalais, or the reformed Egyptian army. Some were keen volunteers, some not. French methods of raising troops in the Western Sudan were often close to slave-raiding, while men of the Congo 'Force Publique' believed that only by obeying the brutal orders of their officers would they ever be allowed home. It was the dedication of officers and ncos which usually determined quality - a point amply demonstrated by contrasting the appallingly demoralised Egyptian armies of 1883-4 with their reformed successors.

European volunteers were raised from settlers in Southern Africa to fight the Zulus, Ndebele and Boers. Enthusiastic and skilled in scoutcraft, the volunteers' knowledge of the terrain and the enemy made them invaluable. They were not, however, amenable to military discipline, and their bigotry towards 'the natives' often involved atrocities. For the 'white man's war' against the Boers the British used metropolitan volunteers such as the yeomanry or the upper-class City Imperial Volunteers, as well as some 25,000 Australians, Canadians and New Zealanders - 'All independent, queer and odd, but most amazin' new'.

Auxiliaries were required in large numbers by the imperial field forces, to serve as scouts, interpreters, drivers, porters and servants. Most of these were local Africans - Bantu ox drovers, Somali camel boys, etc - but specialised services demanded such exotic types as Canadian 'voyageur' boatmen (Nile campaign, 1884-5), Chinese labourers or Indian crews for plate-laying. The Germans even brought New Guinea head-hunters to East Africa! As for porters, even a small expedition like the Ilorin Column (1897) had 488 carriers to 340 combatants. In the First World War the Belgians employed no less than 260,000 Congolese as porters for their East Africa campaign.

The composition of armies. A 'Field Force' was a very variable quantity indeed. De Paiva's Portuguese expedition of 1890 in Angola comprised 20 officers and 550 soldiers - a mix of Angola Askaris, Damara tribesmen and Boer volunteers - plus 50 carts, 2 Krupp guns and 2 machine guns. Such small forces at least made up for lack of numbers by heavy firepower: eg the Gambia expedition of 1894 had 2 pack guns, 2 rocket devices and a Maxim gun supporting 400 men of the West India Regiment and a similar number of porters. In the Jameson Raid of 1896 there were 3 field guns and 8 Maxims to support 494 riders; while at Waterberg in 1904 Von Trotha's 4,000 men had 14 machine guns and no less than 36 field guns. For each 1000 men in these small forces a proportion of 2.5 to 16 machine guns and 3.5 to 9 pieces of artillery was maintained.

In larger forces the firepower was proportionally rather less. At Adowa the 17,700 Italians had 56 guns (or 3.16 per thousand), and in South Africa in January 1900 the 86,730 British had 270 guns (3.1 per thousand). The proportion of cavalry varied more widely according to time and place - eg horsemen were vital in South Africa, but useless in Sierra Leone. But, in general, forces were better balanced and more homogenous when the mission was more important.

Command

Command in Africa demanded a mixture of military skill, political acumen, imaginative improvisation and robust health. Successful leadership depended less on the application of set procedures than on the ability to devise and implement a plan which worked. The effective rule was that there were no rules. Command could devolve onto very junior officers - in the farthest reaches of the Congo or Tchad it was possible for a young subaltern or captain to become the sole authority for the colonial power, wielding immense local influence. This responsibility could become the springboard to promotion and a great reputation; for example the rise of Marshal Joffre dated from 1894 when, as an obscure engineer officer, he found himself in command of a small French column which went on to capture Timbuktu. (He did not see action again until 1914, when he was responsible for more than thirty Army Corps in Northern France!)

An African command could also break a man's nerve or health. Wolseley took quinine for years after a bout of Malaria in Asante, and one Portuguese officer, delirious with fever, shot three inoffensive tribespeople, and then himself, in 1887. Another Portuguese officer committed suicide by wrapping himself in a flag, sitting down amid 14 kegs of powder, and then blowing himself through the roof of his house. Obviously command in Africa was no easy matter.

Lord Methuen leads an infantry attack

The commander in battle had two main options. He would normally involve himself in the thick of the fighting, inspiring his troops by personal example and being present at points of crisis. Stirring deeds were the staple of Victorian myth, and the essence of a regimental officer's duty, but problems arose when more senior officers went too close to the front. At Modder River the British General, Lord Methuen, left his HQ for several hours to lead a platoon attack, thereby abandoning his control over the battle. At Colenso General Buller took command of a battery. This was leadership - but not generalship.

Alternatively a commander might adopt an 'administrative' role and place himself at a more rearward command post where news could be evaluated and plans revised. This was the precursor of the 'chateau generalship' of WW1, although never taken to the same extreme. Most commanders sensibly combined aspects of both styles - eg Wolseley would scout the ground with his staff, then retire to where he could 'read' the progress of the battle. Kitchener - a cool 'administrator' who covered spells of indecision with his icy exterior - successfully 'led from the front' at Omdurman but created chaos; panic and defeat when he tried to do the same at Paardeberg in 1900.

The commander and his army

A commander's relationship with those under his orders was of the utmost importance. If the men had confidence in their leader, they would devote themselves to carrying out the most risky of operations. On the other hand a commander who lost that sense of belief among his army would encounter lethargy and demoralisation. Letters from the Zulu war show bouyant faith in Lord Chelmsford collapsing into dejected apathy after his defeat at Isandhlwana.

An officer could use several approaches to motivate his forces. Lord Roberts was loved by his army for his cheerful interest in, and genuine concern for the soldiers. By contrast Kitchener - who is reported to have never spoken to a private soldier except to issue an order - relied on cool efficiency to win his troops' respect. Negrier was a martinet who won little affection, but his reforms revitalised the Foreign Legion in Algeria in the 1880s. Wolseley's men expected all to go well under his leadership, and 'All Sir Garnet' became a catch phrase for anything that went without a hitch.

British troops in particular wanted their officers to 'muck in' - eg Sir Charles Warren sought popularity by taking very public baths in the middle of his camp! French officers, however, preferred a more grandiose manner. Lyautey held himself more aloof, although he encouraged an inner circle of staff officers, and engaged his men with colourful reminiscences. There were different ways to establish one's 'style of leadership', but without one the troops would lack an image to believe in - a faith that could carry them through in adversity.

The commander and his officers

The development of staff systems in Europe during the late nineteenth century barely touched the armies in Africa. Commanders needed skilled administrators for intelligence, supply transport etc., but often found there was only a mixed collection of enthusiastic yet inexperienced young officers available to perform these tasks. In the Zulu war this brought confusion as innocent subalterns and over-age colonels failed to cope with a land which generally lacked roads, transport and sources of supply. Seasoned campaigners understandably sought to create more reliable staffs for their own use - Gallieni's circle remained in contact with him long after he had retired, and included Lyautey, whose own staff was a huge, adoring group of disciples known as the 'Zaouia' (a type of Moslem religious brotherhood). Wolseley's 'Ring' was an effort both to encourage the ablest young officers and to build an effective team which could be used again and again. This

Troop movements are directed with the help of a heliograph.

group was notable for its keen interest in 'scientific soldiering', at a time when British officers tended to be brave rather than bright. Its members included Generals Butler, Brackenbury, Sir Evelyn Wood and the ill-fated George Pomeroy-Colley. Perhaps its most interesting product of all was Sir Redvers Buller...

Battle in Africa

The commander and his orders

The first duty of a soldier is to obey his orders, and this was never more true than in the Victorian era. At Amba Alagi in 1895 Major Toselli knew his detachment of 2,150 Italian askaris was outnumbered ten or fifteen to one by Ras Makonnen - yet his orders did not permit retreat. He chose to make a stand and died, with most of his command, because obedience was more important than initiative. During the Boer War the energetic Lord Dundonald was repeatedly put 'on the carpet' for exceeding his orders, while a brilliant flanking action by the King's Royal Rifle Corps - which could have prevented the disaster at Spion Kop - was recalled when it was on the verge of success because Buller had not ordered it.

However, some officers chose to disregard orders entirely. Lyautey conducted an elaborate disinformation campaign against his superiors while he was 'digesting' Morocco. He knew there were no accurate maps in Paris, so he would annex a Moroccan town, give it a new name, and say it was in Algeria. However, he brooked no deceit from his own subordinates, and sent home the impulsive Charles Mangin for showing unwanted initiative. The most astonishing disobedience during this period was that of Voulet and Chanoine, two junior French officers whose expedition to Zinder in 1899 became a blood-stained rampage of pillage and slave-raiding. When an officer was sent to relieve Voulet, he was murdered on the orders of his new subordinate. Eventually the Tirailleurs Senegalais mutinied, killed Voulet and Chanoine, and still went on to capture Zinder.

Toselli's last stand.

The commander and the enemy

A commander's attitude towards his adversary affected his whole approach to the campaign. Few Europeans of the period felt much respect or regard for Africans - including Boers - and most considered them debased heathen savages, or worse. This could lead to a casual disregard for basic military precautions, resulting in disasters such as Isandhlwana and Majuba Hill. It could also mean that African lives, rights and property were considered valueless - eg wounded Mahdists could expect no medical attention from the British, and were lucky if they escaped a bayonetting. Kitchener received deserved criticism for this after the wholesale slaughter at Omdurman. Even officers who had some sympathy with Africans, such as Theodor von Leutwein, were carried by white settler opinion to harsh measures against those who dared oppose the Europeans. His successor - the exceedingly ruthless, but not very capable, von Trotha - was so enraged by Herero victories that he put into effect a policy of total extermination which caused the death of some 60,000 people (75% of the tribe).

Mahdist wounded are despatched after Omdurman.

Redvers Henry Buller saw service in China, India and Canada before entering the Army Staff College in 1871. He left his course to serve under Wolseley in Asante - the first of a series of African campaigns that were to place Buller in a wide variety of command positions. He led an irregular cavalry force in the Zulu war, was Chief of Intelligence in Egypt, an infantry brigadier at Suakin, and Wolseley's Chief of Staff during the Nile expedition. In 1899, after fourteen years in staff positions at home, he was given overall command in South Africa. His record was excellent and his reputation high - yet he failed disastrously. Why?

In his person, Buller embodied many of the contradictions of Victorian warfare. He was extremely brave, and won the Victoria Cross for saving his men at Hlobane; but he also proved irresolute and unable to abide by his own decisions. Outwardly bluff and calm, Buller panicked inwardly at Colenso. Devoted to the welfare of his men, he felt unable to risk their lives on a high-stakes gamble - though he knew the troops would do anything he asked. A resourceful staff officer and a heroic fighting soldier, he was ultimately terrified of overall command. He felt secure as an able, active subordinate to Wolseley - but on his own he was out of his depth.

Collecting Supplies

Armies cannot even begin to wage war unless they have provisions and transport. In Africa neither was easily available locally, so they had to be brought. An Italian describing the quays of Massowa evoked the same scenes that were familiar in French Algiers, British Cape Town and a dozen other ports. He spoke of the disembarkation of battalions, the issue of baggage, the shortage of barges and labourers... 'they had to disembark the men, extract the cases of rifles with a crane, embark them on the boats, land them on the beach or quay, open them, take out the rifles, rub off the grease and distribute them, taking away the cases to the warehouse.' Eventually, order emerged out of chaos. Barracks and hospitals were built, and within two or three days each newly-arrived battalion was ready to march.

Transport had to be effective if adequate logistical support was to be guaranteed to the troops. A British battalion had nine tons of basic impedimenta, whixh meant about 17 wagons and carts. In Zululand Lord Chelmsford calculated he would need 1,800 tons of stores to supply 16,000 fighting men for a 6-8 week campaign. His agents scoured South Africa and bought 977 wagons, 56 carts, 10,023 oxen, 803 horses and 398 mules, collecting 90% of the transport beasts and vehicles in Natal. One officer was also sent to Texas to buy 400 mules; others came from Cyprus, Spain and Italy.

Following Bugeaud, Lyautey preferred to load equipment on mules rather than men - but this created a boom in mule prices. British transport officers in upper Egypt in 1885 paid £16 for camels - up to twice the usual price for beasts that were often old or sick - but when they could not procure enough, they searched as far as Aden and Somalia. In the hunt for Morenga, the Germans requested 1,000 camels for pack transport, while in Ethiopia in 1868 the British used no less than 41,723 transport animals - from donkeys to elephants - to support 14,600 soldiers. For the Adowa campaign (1896) the Italians bought 8,200 camels and 3,000 mules in the space of two months.

Ammunition and weapons were, of course, vital. An infantryman could carry 50-70 rounds, or perhaps twice this if he laid aside most of his equipment. The Somaliland Camel Constabulary bore 140 rounds per man, camels being stronger than men, with an extra 160 in reserve on pack animals.

Regimental reserves would normally carry 50-200 rounds per man, with more in an army 'field reserve' (Some 480 rounds per man in the Zulu war). The prodigious rate of fire of modern weapons meant that these figures were really not high. The standard allowance of 3,000 rounds for a Maxim, for instance allowed only five minutes' continuous fire. In 1899 the British in South Africa had stocks of only 200 rounds per field gun, but 151,000,000 rifle cartridges (of which 44% were of the recently banned 'Dum Dum' type) - ie a total of almost 2,000 per man.

Loads carried (in lbs)
A Porter	40-50
An Infantryman	60
A Foreign Legionnaire*	100
A Mule	200
A Camel	300
Heavy Ox Wagon (good terrain)	8,000
Heavy Ox Wagon (bad terrain)	2,000
A Railway Freight Car	40,000+

* The Legion suffered an enormous loss of mobility as the price for this, until 'compagnies montées' were introduced.

Battle in Africa

Tents etcetera A Victorian army required a vast assortment of tackle to operate in Africa. Tents - from two-man triangular models, through the 18-man British bell-tent, to huge marquees - were needed in large numbers. Spare uniforms and boots were required, although troops expected to serve in tatters. Soap, candles, tobacco and firewood were necessities. Luxuries which were usually appreciated sometimes proved a nuisance. In 1885 Brackenbury spent days sorting out coffee-grinders and beer taps from more vital equipment for his River Column.

Drink Water was a basic need. A gallon per man per day was usual, but often much less was available, and animals needed much more. The 6,000 gallons brought for the East Surrey Regiment at Hashin was expected to serve 600 men for four days.

In desert lands the presence of water determined movements and key strategic points. In Algeria and Morocco the French, unable to bring their mobile foes to battle, garrisoned wells and held the 250-mile line of the Zousfana river. In SW Africa the Germans defeated the Herrero only by cordoning them off in the waterless Omakehe waste. Where there was no fresh water, deep wells might be dug, or seawater pumped by condenser apparatus, transferred to iron tanks and then to barrels for transport. In the march to Tofrek (1885) Major de Cossen, staff officer in charge of water supplies, employed 580 camels carrying 11,500 gallons.

Bad water would cripple an army. Enteric fever from contaminated water immobilised Roberts' army after the siege of Paardeberg and capture of Bloemfontein. Soldiers in any case preferred tea, coffee or cocoa to plain water - and alcohol best of all. French troops in Algeria drank Pinard - local red wine - and the white rum known as Tafia. Both Wolseley and Queen Victoria deplored the issue of rum to British soldiers, seeking to substitute jams, pickles and other edibles. Officers still brought their own chosen tipples - eg Sir Evelyn Wood carried 40 cases of wine on the Gordon expedition, while the German staff at Swakopmund in 1904 brought large supplies of champagne and cigars. Whenever possible ice and soda water were also brought to ensure a proper standard of living.

Food. Army rations were often plentiful but seldom good. Here are two examples of daily rations:
British Army, Sudan, 1885
1¼lb fresh, or 1lb preserved, meat
1¼lb bread or 1 lb biscuit
1lb fresh, or 1oz compressed, veg.
Small quantities coffee, tea, sugar, salt, lime-juice and jam or marmalade - Wolseley's 'teetotal' replacement for the half-gill (2½oz) spirit ration of rum usually issued.
Italian Army, Ethiopia, 1896
400 grams meat (451 gr. = 1lb)
200 grams pasta or rice
15 grams oil and cheese
24 cl wine
3 cl rum
Also vegetables, coffee, salt, sugar and bread as available.

Allowances for native troops were usually lower than for Europeans - eg Egyptian soldiers received half the meat allowance of their British comrades, while Aden camel-drivers lived largely on biscuit, dates and onions. As much food as possible would be procured locally to save transport - eg Zulu war letters mention the good quality of the milk, while the column ambushed by the Boers at Bronkhorstspruit (1880) was eating stolen peaches - but most still had to be brought from home. Chicago 'Bully' beef was the Tommy's staple, while the French soldier lived largely on canned sardines. Barrels of pork, boxes of tea or crates of biscuit were bulky and heavy requiring vast baggage trains. Slaughter beeves and sheep had to be ushered along in the army's wake. Officers improved their own lot by bringing delicacies from home - a hamper from Fortnum & Mason's was widely considered essential equipment. The soldiers made do with tinned goods, stringy beef and bread from the field bakeries, 'half of it sand', as Private Davies of the 90th reported.

Forage allowances in the Sudan were:
For English horses: 10lb corn, 12lb hay or chopped straw, 1oz salt.
For Native horses and mules: 8 lb barley, 8 lb chopped straw, ½oz salt.
For Camels: 10lb beans, 15lb chopped straw.
In certain areas the grass was suitable for fodder, but cavalry horses were not trained to graze, and unfamiliar foodstuffs would often upset the delicate constitution of the animals. The loss of horses was massive.

Strategic Mobility

Moving an army in Africa involved massive effort, effective organisation and resourceful improvisation. Some of the available Transport Officers were placed in charge of convoys, others handled the complex detail of servicing the Lines of Communication. A route of march had to be devised that was practical on the ground as well as on the map. Basic survival needs - food, water and healthy camp grounds - had to be made available, and the rugged terrain had to be carefully considered. In desert conditions the 'Night March' might be used to allow rest through the heat of the day - although this entailed risks resulting from confusion and slow progress in the darkness. In tropical rain forests movement was slower still; yet every day that could be saved reduced the level of sickness among the soldiery. Mistakes were common: officers grazed horses on infected pasture, or drowned ox teams in swollen river crossings. Some leaders relied only on a desperate hope that everything would fall into place. Others, such as Sir Charles Warren at the Tugela drifts (1899) missed the 'big picture' through excessive immersion in the details. Trial and error were the watchwords!

An army's movement was based on the speed of its slowest component. Lightly equipped forces could cover great distances when the need arose - Capt Franke's feldkompanie rode almost 200 miles in 100 hours to relieve Okahandja (1904) while the Cape Mounted Police marched 80 miles in 24 hours to catch Morenga in 1907. Foot units could also achieve notable feats of marching - a quality especially prized in the Armée d'Afrique. A Foreign Legion company covered 38 miles in a night march to relieve Taghit (1903), while Lyautey's Algerian irregulars marched 125 miles in 49 hours during the Razzia in 1906. Such rapid marches were, however, exceptional. In heavy country a column with baggage and wheeled artillery might crawl along: the 9 pdr and 12 pdr guns in the Bida-Ilorin campaign of 1897 were hand-hauled at 1 mph. At Suakin Graham's force averaged 1½ mph over the thorny plain to Tofrek in 1885. In mountain or jungle terrain, movement was barely possible: Dodd's column in Dahomey (1892) hacked its way through scrub jungle at only five miles per day.

Transport problems in South Africa 1879

'Average' movement rates (From a 1914 manual, assuming good weather and a much better terrain than anyone could reasonably expect. Field artillery is assumed to equal or exceed infantry rates.)

	Miles per hour (including halts)	Miles per day	Miles per day with forced march
Infantry / Mixed Troops	2½	12 - 16	16-30
Cavalry	3½	20 - 25	25-50
Wagons	2-2½	12 - 20	-

Corporal H Brown of the 2/24th Foot (South Wales Borderers) showed how theory compared with reality in his account of the 74 mile march between Greytown and Helpmakaar in Natal December 1878.

Day	Time	Distance (in miles)	Comments
1	11am - 6pm	16	Leave Greytown, climb a hill 8 miles long.
2	5am - 10am	11	Cross river Mooi then 'all down hill', followed by Christmas dinner of foundered bullocks 'not fit for a dog'.
	3pm - 8pm	12	To the Tugela river.
3	5am - 4pm	-	Cross the Tugela, camp on far bank.
4	4am - 8am	8	Halt for breakfast and dinner, then-
	3pm - 7.30pm	10	To Sandspruit.
5	-	-	Rest day at Sandspruit.
6	5am - 5pm	17	Up a steep hill to Helpmakaar.

Total: 74 or 12.3 miles per day average.

During the same campaign an officer of the Naval Brigade wrote that "Our usual routine is as follows: 4 am strike tents, breakfast 5.30, leave camp; halt about 10 for dinner, when the oxen are outspanned for two hours; start again at the pm, and camp by some river in the evening".

Battle in Africa

Flying columns were fast-moving forces carrying their own supplies. Some of them really did enjoy enormous mobility - eg British Mounted Infantry units of the second Boer War eventually met the Commando on its own terms. French Sahariens harnessed the mobility of the desert Arab: working in tandem with bodies of Goumiers (irregular horse and foot) and Turcos, these troops were the leading exponents of the Razzia.

Many flying columns, however, became weighed down by their own supplies - eg the Germans in Tanganyika and SW Africa found it difficult to move away from the railway. Without magazines to fall back on, a flying column which got into difficulties and lost its supplies would be entirely deprived of resources. In 1881 the Flatters expedition ran out of food and water, and had to make a nightmare retreat harassed by the Tuareg. In 1883 Hicks Pasha combined both problems when his force had too much baggage for rapid movement, but too little food or water to survive the ensuing delays.

'Melik' in action on the Nile in 1898.

Boats were by far the easist way to travel in much of Africa. Local vessels might be used - the Nuggurs and Gyassas of the Nile, or the canoes of tropical Africa - but these were soon supplemented by steamers on the great lakes, on the Nile and on the Niger. There were also collapsible boats such as the 'Faidherbe' carried to Fashoda by the Marchand expedition, which broke down into sections for porterage. For the Gordon expedition 800 whaleboats were commissioned, each built to carry 12 men with rations for 100 days. With a draught of 2 feet and a pair of masts they could negotiate the dangerous cateracts when guided by their crew of bluejackets, West African 'Kroomen' or even Canadian 'Voyageurs' (the best of whom were Iroquois).

Civilian steamers might be armoured with sandbags, timber and boilerplating. At Khartoum, Gordon's defence depended largely on his small flotilla of improvised gunboats, but purpose-built vessels were often used elsewhere. These varied from tiny steam launches, through the 'Tamai' class sternwheelers of 1885 (carrying a 9 pdr and two machine guns, with a speed over 11 knots), to the powerful screw-driven 'Melik' class cruisers, which carried searchlights, two 12 pdr quick-firing guns, a 4 inch howitzer and four Maxims.

Armoured train, Egypt 1882

Railways were the quickest and most reliable means of transport for men and equipment. In 1879 there were few lines in Africa, most of them close to the northern and southern coasts; but the later conquests of imperialism were more widely supported by an extension of the rails. By 1890 the Algerian system had grown from only 300 miles to reach into Tunisia, and a trans-Sahara line was planned. The Niger-Senegal line was begun in the 1880s and completed in 1904; meanwhile the Capetown-Kimberly line was opened, and the Natal railway extended to Ladysmith.

Armies often tied their operations closely to the railways - eg Methuen's 1899 campaign to relieve Kimberley, or the Germans' precarious advance across the Namib desert. (They only had one narrow-gauge train per day, with 6 cars each carrying only 5 tons; but without this tiny lifeline they would have been unable to conduct the campaign at all.) Where there was no line, the military might seek to build one - eg the abortive Suakin-Berber railway attempted in 1885, or Kitchener's 'artery of iron' (the Sudan Military Railway) in 1896. The latter ran 230 miles between Wadi Halfa and Abu Hamed. It was laid at the unusually rapid rate of $2-2\frac{1}{2}$ miles per day, thanks to the excellent planning of the Canadian engineer Lt Girouard and the skilled work of his highly-motivated 'Railway battalion'. The Uganda railway, by contrast, took five years to cover 580 miles - delayed in part by the regularity with which platelayers were eaten by lions. Once a line was in service, the trains could move between 200 and 400 miles in a day provided progress was not slowed by breakdowns, trackwork or administrative delays.

Reconnaissance and Signals

Reconnaissance duties were the work of light, mobile forces operating as a screen ahead, and on either side of the main force. The scouts could be:
1 Regular troops, mounted on horse or camel - or on foot in close terrain. Regulars had the advantage of discipline and standard procedures, but often failed to recognise important signs of the enemy, and generally had relatively poor moblilty and fieldcraft skills.
2 Locally-raised irregulars, such as the excellent Basuto horsemen of the Natal Native Horse, or the North African Goumiers. Accustomed to local conditions and fleet of foot, irregulars could bring in useful information. But their overall efficiency was often impaired by indiscipline and a predilection for private raiding.
3 Scouts, spies and guides hired specially for the job - not as soldiers. Selected by intelligence officers for their keen fieldcraft and knowledge of the region, these scouts were potentially the most effective of all the three categories of reconnaissance troops. They were attuned to the 'Bush Telegraph' - that network of news and rumour which connected African communities - and could be astonishingly perceptive and useful to an intelligence officer who handled them properly. However, regular officers frequently failed to make use of these resourceful but 'unmilitary' agents.
4 Balloons had first been used for observation at Fleurus in 1793, and later in the American Civil War; but they encountered much resistance in European armies. Major Templer pioneered a balloon made of goldbeaters' skin, and commanded a detachment at Suakin in 1885. Sadly for him, however, his efforts were neutralised by high winds and thorny vegetation. Methuen's and Buller's armies took captive balloons with them in 1899, following Warren's failure to use this method to study the topography of the Spion Kop area, and at Ladysmith Col. Rawlinson ascended to 1,600 feet, noting "I found it difficult to spot the guns as the balloon rocks about and keeps revolving so much that one cannot keep one's glasses steady."

Inflating the bag was a slow process, so filled balloons would be towed along above a moving column. French soldiers serving in Morocco referred to it as 'the betrayer', since its appearance on the horizon would alert the enemy in plenty of time. By 1911 the balloon had a rival in aerial reconnaissance duties: the Italians used powered aircraft in support of their forces in Libya, as did Lyautey in Morocco from 1912.

Navigation in Africa demanded great care. During the night march to Tel El Kebir a naval officer with a compass led the advance. During a similar moonlit operation at Magersfontein in 1899 a misjudgment of distance took the Highland Brigade to within 400 yards of Boer lines while still in close column. At Colenso local guides led Hart's brigade into the loop of an unfordable river - then ran away! Treachery on the part of guides was always a possibility, and hostages were often taken to ensure honest dealing. Where possible a path of advance was carefully planned beforehand, with staff officers drawing maps and views of the terrain to be covered. One such officer was Lt. Jahleel Carey, who accompanied the French Prince Imperial's reconnaissance of possible camping grounds in Zululand in June 1879. Carey was lucky to escape unscathed from the ambush which claimed the Prince's life and caused a European political scandal.

By 1899 some photographic units were available to help terrain analysis, although they were used mainly to reproduce existing maps.

Intelligence. In European armies, permanent intelligence departments were a recent development, and the British, for example, scarcely possessed one at all: their mapping department had 30 members compared to 230 in the French, and in 1899 its budget was 6.6% that of the German. In Africa all the colonial powers relied on improvised intelligence structures - some remarkably efficient, but all ignored and disdained by the 'fighting soldiers'. The French and Italians emphasised the administrative and political roles of the Intelligence Officer. The men of the 'Bureaux Arabes' became minor kingmakers, by wheeling and dealing with local Caids for information and military assistance. In Morocco Major Simon became a master of intrigue between competing Berber chieftains; in Eritrea General Arimondi had established a spy network of informant villagers and selected Askari accompanying each column. This was a double-edged game, and on one occasion his escort discovered two informers hiding in readiness to tell the Ethiopians of the General's presence.

In the Mahdist state there was a complex and effective network of informers and travelling agents run by Sir Reginald Wingate. He used a team of Lebanese interpreters to process reams of information, which he compressed into his book 'Mahdism in the Egyptian Sudan' (1891) - a brilliant work and a propaganda coup. Wingate was encouraged by his superior, Kitchener, who in turn had once served in a convincing Arab disguise as a liason officer between the besieged Gordon and the authorities in

Battle in Africa

The heliograph, shown here being used in 1879, replaced the heliostat - with a fixed mirror - which was adopted by the British Army in 1875. It was carried by all major, and many minor forces throughout our period. Use of the instrument reached its peak of efficiency during the Boer War, when speeds of up to 16 words per minute were attained.

Signals had improved greatly during the nineteenth century:
1 The electric telegraph linked Europe with its settlements in Africa. In 1862 St Louis de Senegal was joined to Dakar. In Gordon's time a line ran London-Cairo-Khartoum to Rejjaf on the upper Nile, and by 1914 it extended to Mombasa. By 1870 the Royal Engineers had a field telegraph section, of which a detachment linked Suakin to Tofrek for the 1885 campaign. The telegraph was slow to lay and easy to cut. It could not be relied upon when guerillas threatened rear security - eg in the Boer and Hereros/Hottentot campaigns.
2 The telephone was as yet barely used in warfare. Johannesburg had an exchange in 1895, but the military value of the telephone (eg a link to a balloon observer) was hardly recognised. The same was true of radio, although the French had established wireless links with some of their outlying forts in Morocco by 1914.
3 The heliograph was essentially a hinged mirror on a tripod, which could flash a coded message on a cloudless day when there was intervisibility. The British 14.137" model had a range of 90 miles, the 7.087" model 48 miles.
4 Semaphore flags were easily carried, but could be seen over only a short distance, even in the best visibility.
5 Oil burning lamps with focussing lenses could transmit signals a long way - up to 150 miles with one French model - but suffered from many of the same limitations as the heliograph. At Spion Kop the beleagured troops had a lamp... but no oil could be found!

Cairo. In the Transvaal the work of Aubrey Woolls-Sampson and his ring of African agents made Benson's column the scourge of the Boer guerillas. Fiercely loyal to his men, who risked execution if captured, Woolls-Sampson seemed able to predict exactly where a commando would be at any time. Eventually the Boers were forced to unite several commandos under Louis Botha to wipe out Benson in October 1901.

Successful intelligence officers were often renegades, more at home in kraal or casbah than at regimental dinners. Their stock-in-trade was an understanding of African culture and an ability to work with alien peoples, not the finer points of European etiquette.

Runners and riders often carried despatches, although they were slow by comparison with heliograph or wire. A 1914 manual gave despatch riders' speeds as 'Ordinary - 5mph; Rapid - 7 to 8 mph; Urgent - 10 to 12 mph', and unmounted messengers may have been able to sustain only half of that. However, human messengers did have advantages of adaptability over their faster mechanical counterparts. Gordon used volunteers to carry despatches out of besieged Khartoum (although nobody wanted to come back with a reply!). One resourceful Arab irregular brought news to a French force by joining a charge of Moroccan cavalry, then dropping his rifle and leaping over the amazed French line.

It was usual to send at least two men separately to carry each message.

At Spion Kop Col. Thorneycroft did not know that he was in command until several hours after his appointment: one runner was killed at his feet, while the other became involved in leading a rush of reinforcements. He recieved the news only when a subaltern who had seen the heliograph yelled "You are a general".

17

March Security

Once deployed for battle, the Europeans could usually defeat their African opponents by superior organisation and firepower. On the march or in camp, however, the story was different: African fieldcraft and local knowledge could be used to achieve surprise, while darkness or natural cover could be exploited to negate the technical advantages of the Imperial troops. Security on the march and in camp was therefore a key issue for the Europeans. If the procedures failed, the vulnerability of a column or an encampment might easily lead to disaster.

All-round defence was a necessity for any marching force in Africa, in contrast to normal practice in Europe. Four-sided formations (squares of anything from company to brigade size) were adopted, with scouts on all sides. The French divided their columns into a 'fighting square' in front and a 'convoy square' in support, rather than place all the troops and transport in a single large quadrangle. For open terrain Callwell advocated a system of double vedettes at 500-1,500 yards to combat the swift moving warriors of desert or grassland areas. For close country he preferred a variant of the square, using parallel columns linked by front and rear screens of skirmishers. Wolseley used this method against an Asante ambush at Amoaful in 1874.

These measures were complex and time-consuming. One officer who had served in the 1898 'Hut Tax War' in Sierra Leone stated that if he had to write an exam paper on forest campaigning he would discuss the use of flankers and advance guards but, since they would reduce progress to about a mile a day in thick bush, he would not use them. Instead, knowing that the only real danger would lie in stumbling upon a concealed stockade, he would send ahead a group of 'friendlies'. These would not fight, or even report back, but would be found 'squatting beside the track wearing an expression of deep melancholy'. This would indicate that a stockade lay ahead. Otherwise useless, their sensitivity to the 'bush telegraph' made them invaluable.

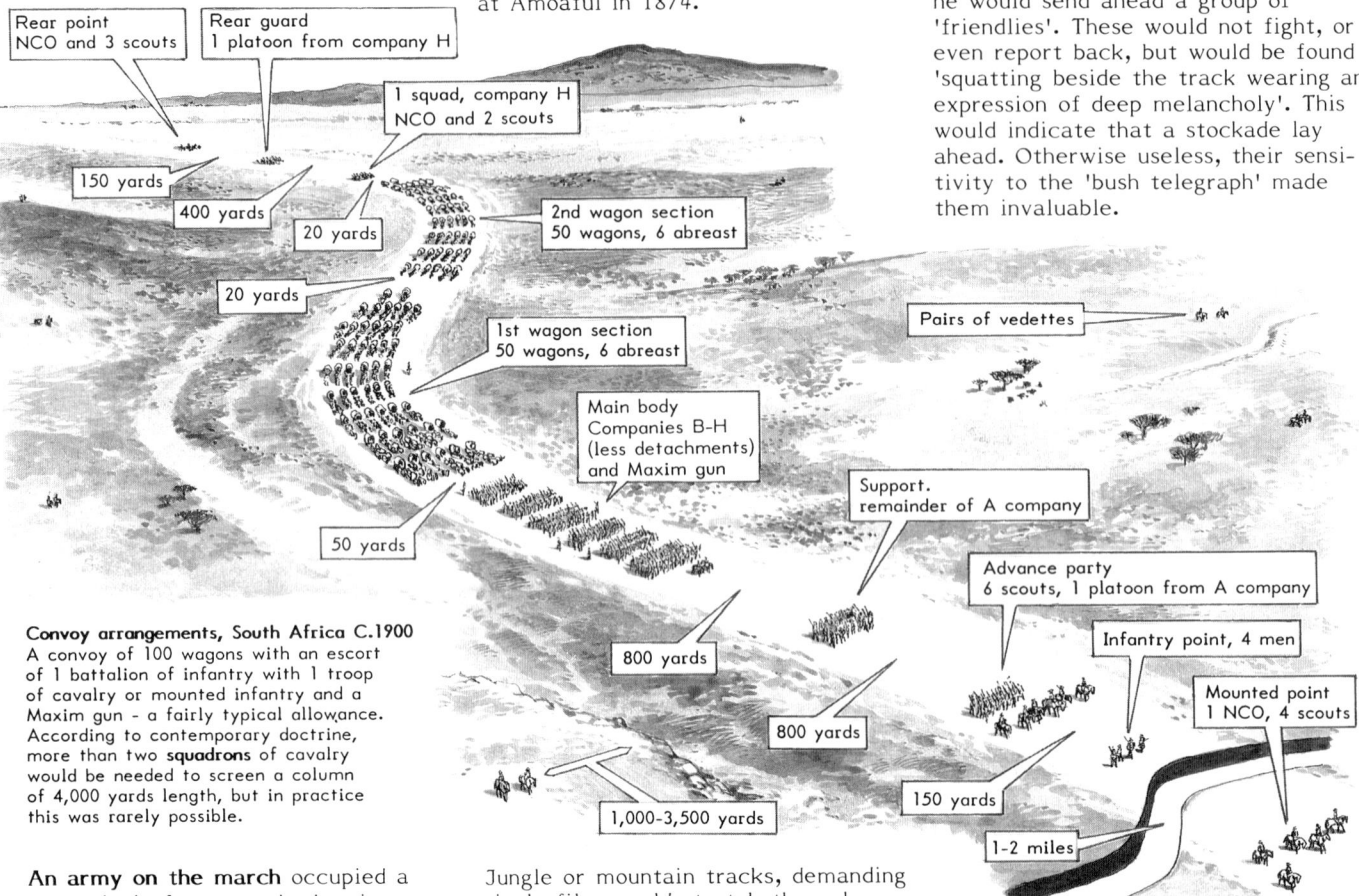

Convoy arrangements, South Africa C.1900
A convoy of 100 wagons with an escort of 1 battalion of infantry with 1 troop of cavalry or mounted infantry and a Maxim gun - a fairly typical allowance. According to contemporary doctrine, more than two **squadrons** of cavalry would be needed to screen a column of 4,000 yards length, but in practice this was rarely possible.

Labels on diagram:
- Rear point: NCO and 3 scouts — 150 yards
- Rear guard: 1 platoon from company H — 400 yards
- 1 squad, company H: NCO and 2 scouts — 20 yards
- 2nd wagon section: 50 wagons, 6 abreast — 20 yards
- 1st wagon section: 50 wagons, 6 abreast — 50 yards
- Main body: Companies B-H (less detachments) and Maxim gun
- Pairs of vedettes
- Support: remainder of A company — 800 yards
- Advance party: 6 scouts, 1 platoon from A company — 800 yards
- Infantry point, 4 men — 150 yards
- Mounted point: 1 NCO, 4 scouts — 1,000-3,500 yards / 1-2 miles

An army on the march occupied a great deal of space, whether it was extended in column or arranged in camp. The following 1914 figures optimistically assume a column of fours at the start of a march, and one night camps on healthy, level ground.

Jungle or mountain tracks, demanding single file, would stretch the column to four times this length for infantry and make wheeled vehicles unusable. (All distances in yards, all vehicles horse drawn.):

Unit	Length of Column	Camping Space
Infantry Brigade: 2,000 men + regimental trains (24 vehicles)	c. 1,300	160 x 200
Cavalry Brigade: 1250 men + regimental trains (26 vehicles)	c. 1,800	200 x 200
Horse-drawn Battery: 6 guns & limber teams, 10 other vehicles	c. 600	150 x 150
Mountain Battery: 6 guns on pack mules	c. 440	75 x 100
Army Transport (per 10 vehicles)	c. 375	110 x 110

African conditions usually called for many more animals and vehicles than were needed in Europe - eg a British battalion needed four carts and five wagons at home, but seventeen ox-wagons for Natal service in 1879. When a spanned ox-wagon took up 60 yards of column, only thirty of them in single file would cover a mile. In any march, also, a column would 'stretch' up to 25% - or much more if it fell into disorder. Likewise a permanent camp needed more acreage than a one-day halt, if the force was to stay healthy.

Battle in Africa

Camp security demanded a compact defensive perimeter; but sanitary requirements demanded a more open plan.

```
Reserve
            Supports          Sentry squads
  ⬜——c.1,000 yards——⬜          or 'Cossack posts'
                      \        ○
                       \  c.800 yards     ○
A squadron of cavalry   \                ○
can cover 3,500 yards    ●——Pickets——●   Patrols  °°°
                              c.400 yards  \ 40 yards
A battalion of infantry                    ○
can cover 2,500 yards                   Sentries or Vedettes  °°°
```

As a general rule latrines and cooking areas would be on opposite sides, with easy access to water and fuel. Men would draw water upstream of the animals. The perimeter lines might be guarded by trenches, thorn zarebas or wagon laagers. Beyond the camp lines were outposts - as much as 5,000 yards distant for a large camp threatened by artillery; or as little as 1-200 yards for a small force facing a stealthy infantry opponent.

Outposts took up 10-30% of the total force in theory, although under campaign conditions and with differing terrain there were wide variations.

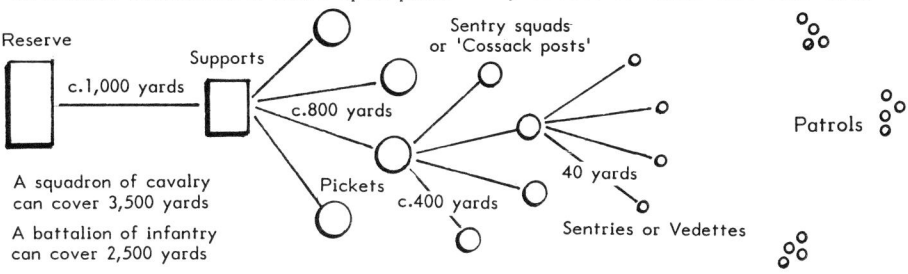

El Moungar. The Dangers to a marching column are illustrated by the French defeat at El Moungar, in Morocco, on 2nd September 1903. A convoy of 3,000 camels carrying supplies for the fortified post at Taghit was divided into three echelons, in an attempt to minimise the risk if they were attacked. Captain Vauchez led the second echelon of 600 camels escorted by his mounted company of the 2nd Legion Etrangère. It left El Morra at 2am and reached the convoy halt of El Moungar at 9.30. As the Legionnaires began breakfast they were attacked from a line of dunes by some 5,000 Berbers and Shaamba Arabs. The camels and mounted company's mules stampeded, splitting the column into three isolated groups of men. Vauchez was mortally wounded; Lt Selchauhansen formed an improvised square. Rifle fire was picking off his soldiers, so he led them in a charge to clear the dunes, but fell with half of his twenty men. Badly wounded, he directed the fire as a sergeant rallied the square to beat off another attack. For eight hours the remnant of the company held out; at 5.30 the third echelon was sighted and the Moroccans withdrew with their booty. Of 113 legionnaires, 34 were killed and 47 wounded: both the officers died the following day.

Sickness claimed more victims than did wounds, and the job of the medical officer - the 'Linseed Lancer' - was difficult. New medicines like quinine could control malaria, and innovations like the hospital ship or the camel or donkey-borne litter might also help; but the key elements in avoiding massive epidemics were clean water and rapid completion of operations. In the Italian march to Adigrat (1896), with good water and a cool, dry atmosphere, the sick rate was 1½%. In Asante, by contrast, the 1874 expedition had a rate of 71% - only six out of more than forty fatalities amongst officers dying of their wounds - despite careful planning and high speed. The French Madagascar campaign (1895) had the most daunting losses from sickness: out of 20,000 men, 20 died in action and 5,735 of 'other causes'.

Animals were even more at risk than men. The British used 500,000 horses in the Great Boer War, of which two-thirds died, mostly from sickness. A third of the 150,000 mules also succumbed. Lt Courtenay of the 20th Hussars in Zululand wrote of the horse sickness, " It is an extraordinary complaint; they begin to flag, and there is a running at the nostrils, and within three hours of these symptoms a strong healthy horse is dead." Dead animals were almost impossible to dispose of adequately, and might in turn bring epidemics to an encamped force.

Night attacks were particularly feared by the Europeans. During the Zulu War a piquet of the 91st Foot fired on 'Zulus' in the morning mist and found themselves in a fire-fight with a trench party of the 60th Rifles. In June 1879 a similar panic, escalating to battalion volleys and artillery fire against an imaginary foe, wounded five men. The Tirailleurs Algériens were notorious for shooting at any sound or movement. Such nervousness was well-founded, for a night or dawn attack could bring disaster. At Dogba in Dahomey (1892) a French camp was stormed at daybreak by 4,000 Fon warriors - lion and elephant hunters assisted by Behanzin's famous Amazons. Snipers had taken position in trees, and began a plunging fire into the bivouac while the warriors mounted charge after charge. The Legionnaires regained the camp by bayonet assault, then held out for four hours until a gunboat arrived to disperse the attackers. Less fortunate was the British laager at Intombi Drift (1879), which was attacked and wiped out as the garrison awoke, so swift was the Zulu attack.

The African Response

African choices, in face of a European invasion, included the following:
1. To oppose the newcomers by military means.
2. To ally with the Europeans against other African peoples.
3. To submit to conquest now, making the best possible terms, to avoid a worse fate later.
4. To avoid the threat by flight.

An African state might select one or more of these options at different times or it might try to 'feel the opposition', by diplomatic means, while delaying the crucial decision. If opinion was divided in council, or if the nature and strength of the new European arrivals was unclear, prevarication appeared to be the best policy. The Tuareg regarded their treaties with the French purely as pauses in a continuing skirmish. Indeed, since the Europeans had little regard for African claims of sovereignty, honest negotiation was of small value. The Ndebele mission to London in 1889, and Prempeh of Asante's delegation of 1896, received scant results for their efforts. The Italians brought Ras Makonnen to Rome less to talk about treaty rights than to impress their might upon him. All this won time - but eventually the Africans would be forced to make a decision. Very often it was to fight.

Mobilising an army might demand lengthy negotiations. Samuel Maherero wrote letters to the chiefs of other SW African peoples - the Ovambos and Hottentots - in order to unite old enemies against the Germans. Samori worked for an alliance with the Tukolor against the French, while Mushidi of the Lunda joined with the Chokwe, an old foe, to combat the Congo Free State (1905-12). If an effective force could be put together, it then had to be held together - no easy task.

The methods of bringing warriors to a gathering point were various. In Ethiopia the Negus ordered a proclamation to be read in the market places, giving time and place of assembly, while the rolls were beaten on the Negarit (great war drums) to remind every man of his duty to serve. The Zulu system of military kraals meant that mobilisation involved simply a calling together of the regiments: in 1879 Cetshwayo summoned the Impis to Ulundi for orders, then sent them to oppose Chelmsford's advance. Boer mobilisation was uncomplicated: the men took their state-issue Mauser rifles with eight day's supplies, and rode to a local rendezvous chosen by their Field-Cornet. Ad hoc arrangements might provide trains to take them to the front, or alternatively they might drive to war with their wives and children in great ox-wagons.

African military systems were as varied as African peoples, but they may be grouped into three main categories:

1. **'Traditional - Formal'**: Rigid and established systems such as the feudal kitet of Ethiopia, the permanent militia of Ijebu and other Yoruba states, or the age-group-set hierarchies of the southern Bantu. The best known of these is the Zulu regimental structure welded together into a military state by Shaka (d.1828), but other Nguni peoples spread the system into Central and East Africa.
2. **'Traditional - Informal'**: The military organisation of less centralised peoples relied on local or customary procedures. A Moroccan Harka would be formed of a number of groups owing loyalty to regional Caids; the Boer Commandos were independent, local forces. Commanding these armies made great demands on their leaders.
3. **'Adapted Modern'**: Egypt and Madagascar had armies trained, drilled and dressed in the European manner. Samori and Ahmadu had trained, uniformed infantry of good quality, while Mutesa of Buganda had added 1,000 musket-armed nobles to his army by 1872. The Amazons of Dahomey were created as a standing elite force; the Boers added drilled artillerymen to their traditional Commandos.

The size of armies varied greatly. In 1902 the Ahaggar Tuareg lost 93 out of 300 warriors when they were defeated by the French - a crushing blow to the tiny manpower of their northern confederation. By contrast the Ethiopian army at Adowa numbered at least 100,000 men - the result of effective mobilisation of a densely populated region. The following survey gives an idea of army size:
Nupe 1897 : 25-30,000
Ijebu 1892 : 7-10,000
Dahomey 1889 : 12,000 (including 4,000 regulars)
Gungunhama's army at Coolela 1896 : 6-10,000
Samori's army 1887 : 30-35,000 'Sofas' (infantry), 3,000 cavalry
Boers at Magersfontein 1899 : 8,000
Boers at Ladysmith 1899 : 12,000
Hereros 1904 : 6-8,000
Hottentots 1904 : 1,500

Battle in Africa

Strategy and supply. The organisational aspects of campaigning - supply, communication etc. - tended to be poor in African armies. Zulu logistics involved Udibi boys travelling with each Impi - 12 - 15 year olds carrying grain, water and sleeping mats. They helped the army to be light and mobile, but they did not always prevent it from starving: at Kambula the Zulu force had not eaten for three days. Equally the Ethiopian army moved from valley to valley like locusts, eating up local stores of food and then moving on. Babikr Bedri recalled serving with Nejumi's starving army in 1889, chewing on date stones and buying the meat of dead camels at extortionate prices. Even when times were good he lived on beans, dates and unground millet. Other supplies than food also ran short - eg some Boer Commandos wore captured British uniforms, despite the risk of being shot, while others wore animal skins.

Mobility and intelligence were the strong points of African armies. Callwell said that they would usually know in advance what the regulars were planning (the 'bush telegraph' was a remarkable instrument indeed!), while strategic mobility was also high. Zulus could move fifty miles a day, crossing rivers by linking arms and rushing into the water.

Strategy was generally simple, relying on local knowledge and effective information-gathering rather than on complex manoeuvres. Some commanders - Menelik, Samori, Jan Smuts, Samuel Maherero - did use elaborate plans, but normally it was the tested policies of guerilla warfare, dogged defence and rapid approach which worked best. Finesse was hard to pull off - but speed and surprise were second nature to African peoples.

A Zulu Impi assembles in open, rolling terrain.

Religion played a key role in preparing African societies to face the European threat. Traditional religions viewed the invasions as a form of witchcraft, an unnatural imbalance in the structure of the universe, and the powers of religious leaders were used to unite and support the warriors. The massive human sacrifices made at Benin in 1897 was therefore less an exercise in wanton bloodshed - as the Europeans saw it - than a desperate effort to invoke divine help against conquest. More often, religion served as a force to overcome tribal divisions: the 'War Charm' cults of Madagascar and the Congo, the Mwari movement of the Shona prophets and the Maji-Maji revolt were all instances of traditional beliefs serving as a focus for resistance to colonial rule. Several cults - including Maji-Maji - promised that enemy bullets would turn to water and that ancestors would return. That this did not come to pass should not blind us to the tremendous vitality and moral strength which religious ideas contributed to the Africans' resistance. Without the support of prophets the Tanganyika peoples could not have set aside their differences, nor could the Ndebele and Shona have come together.

Islam provided a focus for the military efforts of Moslem peoples. Without the charismatic appeal and religious prestige of Bou Amana there would have been no Algerian rising in 1881 to unite the tribes. The concept of the Jihad (Holy War) brought unity when employed effectively by, eg the Sudanese Mahdi (1881-5) and by Al-Sayyid, the 'Mad Mullah' of Somalia (1897-1920).

The Mahdi

Closing with the Enemy

Closing for battle was a time of high excitement and tension for both sides. Europeans would write letters home and make arrangements with comrades in case of death in combat. Africans would undertake prescribed rituals according to their religion, cleansing themselves before facing death. Scouts would bring reports; commanders would analyse information and finalise plans; rumours would run through the ranks. A good first-hand account of the time immediately before battle was written by Lt Graf von Arnim, commander of a patrol probing deep into Hereroland in the summer of 1904: "It gradually grew lighter and we again sent out flank patrols. A magnificent vista opened before us... There was some evidence of the enemy in the midst of this peace of God in nature. There was smoke in the air... from the fires of the Hereros encamped along the base of the little Waterberg... our position was not very secure. If we had been discovered and Samuel decided to cut off our retreat, we would have been in the soup... Everyone congratulated us on our patrol. We had been in the very midst of the Herero camp."

Drawing a blank: Sometimes the invading Europeans were unable to bring their enemy to battle. They would slowly work their way across the landscape 'feeling' for the opposition, and eating up their own stores, while the Africans made themselves scarce. The expedition would return to base tired and despondent. In harsh environments the troops would suffer: thorn bushes and thirst could defeat a column as completely as an ambush, and at far less cost. In SW Africa, Morocco and the Sudan the losses from heat exhaustion on the march were serious. A contemporary history tells us of a march, made by Graham's command several days after the battle of Tamai, that accomplished nothing but proved more expensive (in the short term) than the battle itself: "...between 300 and 400 men fell out of the ranks. There were numerous cases of sunstroke... the number of men who fell out was equal to one-fourth of the whole force, the rear of which, it is said, resembled a routed army. Many of the sick found room in the ambulances, and others trudged along as best they could on foot. The men were becoming tired and disgusted... there was a good deal of grumbling and dissatisfaction in the ranks." This disgust at 'drawing a blank' could demoralise an army and raise serious questions at home. Von Trotha was recalled in 1905 after his attempts to bring the Hottentots to battle failed in a series of converging attacks that met no resistance, but wore out his forces.

War correspondents, artists and, later, photographers were sent out by the new popular press to bring the news of Imperial campaigns home to European firesides. Writers such as Archibald Forbes, G A Henty and Bennet Burleigh gave readers the 'purple prose' they wanted, tales of clean-limbed heroes and savage foes - often turning their despatches into entertaining books (of varying factual accuracy). The young Winston Churchill supplemented his subaltern's pay with commissions from the press, and raised some eyebrows by his comments on Kitchener in 'The River War' (1899). The doyen of the war correspondents was G W Steevens, 'The High Priest of Imperialism', who died of enteric fever during the siege of Ladysmith.

The soldiers regarded correspondents with mixed feelings. Wolseley said they contributed nothing and ate valuable rations; yet he made sure that pressmen had every opportunity to see him in his element. When Sir Garnet fell off his mount before Tel El Kebir, the artist Melton Prior hastened to assure him that he had not even seen the incident!

Prior accompanied Graham's force at Tamai. In his book 'Campaigns of a War Correspondent' he relates how in the late afternoon of 12th March he asked Graham if it was wise to have left so late as to be coming up to the enemy in the dark. Graham replied, "Oh dear, yes; that is all right; we are British troops."

Tamai 1884
march to contact an example

Baker's Zareba

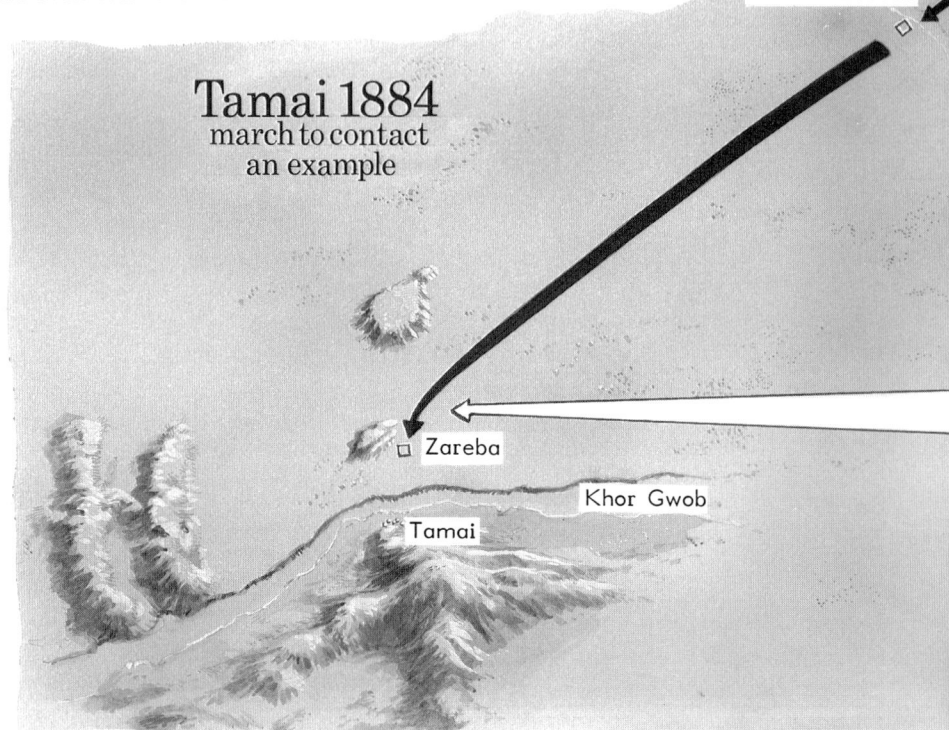

Zareba

Khor Gwob

Tamai

Battle in Africa

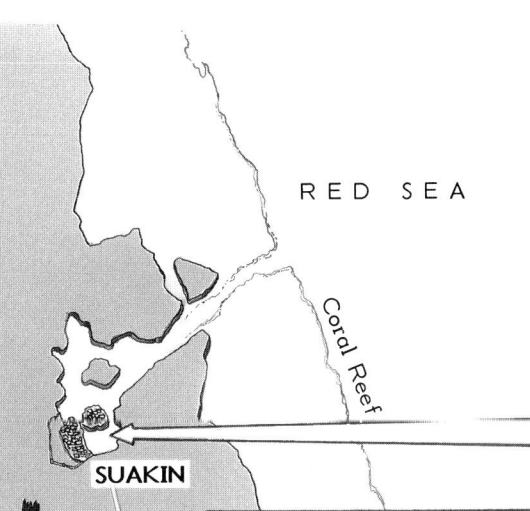

GRAHAM'S FORCE AT TAMAI
Buller's First Brigade
Gordon Highlanders (712) Royal Irish Fusiliers (343) King's Royal Rifle Corps (565) Royal Engineers (62) 8 guns (camel-mounted 7 pounders)
Davis' Second Brigade
Black Watch (623) York & Lancasters (435) Royal Marines (478) Naval Brigade (6 machine guns) 4 guns (9 pounders)
Stewart's Cavalry Brigade
10th Hussars (251) 19th Hussars (362) Mounted Infantry (124)
Total: 3,955 excluding gunners, staff, train etc.

March 9th
Morning. Force disembarks at Suakin. Black Watch sent on to 'Baker's Zareba', 8 miles towards Tamai. Arrive 1300 after a difficult march with many cases of heatstroke.

March 10th & 11th
Supplies pushed on to Baker's Zareba from Suakin. At 18.00 March 11th 1st and 2nd Infantry Brigades leave Suakin for the Zareba, arrive 2400.

March 12th
06.00 Sir Herbert Stewart arrives with the Cavalry Brigade.
10.00 Scouts report enemy in strength 6 miles distant. Graham orders a general advance after dinner.
13.00 The force advances in two brigade squares in echelon with scouts ahead and the main body of cavalry in reserve.
14.00 Scouts report the low hills some 6 miles ahead are clear of enemy. Graham decides to press on with all haste.
15.30 Scouts reach the highest point of the hills and report that the Tamai valley is immediately ahead.
16.00 Infantry reach the base of the ridge, halt while scouts advance further, then continue.
17.00 Scouts report about 4,000 enemy advancing to attack. The force halts in the Tamai valley and starts building a Zareba from thorn bushes. Enemy fire a few rifle shots and appear in numbers 1,200 yards away. They retire when fired on by two 9 pounders and a Gardner gun.
18.00 Nightfall. The cavalry return to Baker's Zareba to water the horses. The rest of the force remains.
21.00 All lights extinguished.

March 13th
00.45 Enemy starts a sporadic dropping fire, with 'excursions and alarums to keep the regulars from sleeping. This continues all night: 1 man killed, 5 wounded.
06.00 At daybreak a 9 pounder and a Gardner are run out to disperse enemy concentrations at about 1,300 yards. Breakfast.
07.00 Stewart arrives with the cavalry.
07.30 Stewart sends Mounted Infantry ahead to reconnoitre enemy position.
08.00 The entire force advances, with Graham accompanying Davis' 2nd Brigade. General Buller follows 800 yards to the right rear with his 1st Brigade, the cavalry deployed behind Davis' square. Ahead a series of low ridges can be seen within a mile; a broken plateau slopes upwards to the high ground. Graham has been told that the bulk of Osman Digna's forces will be concealed in a deep khor - a dry watercourse - across the front of the ridgeline. The morning is bright and clear, and very still.

The Battle of Tamai

08.20 The 2nd Brigade halts to dress its ranks because the rocky terrain has disordered the square. This gives the 1st Brigade, which has started late, a chance to close up to 700 yards distance. The Mounted Infantry are reinforced by two squadrons of cavalry and some Ethiopian irregulars. The Scouts become hotly engaged, Captain Humphreys reports a ravine filled with 'Dervishes'.

08.30 The squares advance: the ravine is 900 yards ahead. Some 5-600 Sudanese can be seen clustered beyond the riverbed. They open an irregular, inaccurate fire.

09.00 As the 2nd Brigade comes within 200 yards of the Khor, the Mahdists make a series of minor assaults. These are beaten off by rifle fire.

09.30 -09.40 The thrust of the Mahdist assault throws the York and Lancasters back onto the Royal Marines behind them. Small knots of soldiers fight back-to-back, with officers attempting to form a firing line. "At this dire crisis the dark and demon-like figures of the foe could be seen rushing on, unchecked even for a moment by the hail of bullets", wrote Burleigh of the 'Telegraph'. The broken square is pushed back 6-800 yards, but morale holds... barely.

Meanwhile a second wave of charging Africans threatens to sweep over Buller's 1st Brigade as it advances towards the ravine. The Brigade halts, s, and cuts down the Mahdists with deliberate volleys. As the attack falters, Buller calmly advances to support his comrades of the 2nd Brigade in their moment of crisis.

09.15 As the attacks die down, Graham orders the Black Watch - comprising the left front half-face of the square - to charge. To their right the York and Lancasters join in the rush forward. The sides of the square receive no order - it is like 'taking the lid off a box', as the front face pulls away from its supports. Reaching a point 30 yards from the ravine, the soldiers open an excited, uncontrolled fire as Hadendowah tribesmen appear from folds in the ground.

09.25 Several thousand Hadendowah converge in an all-out attack on the square, now wreathed in smoke and its ranks in disorder. The Gatling and Gardner guns are rushed to the front, but are unable to halt the charge. A Gardner jams and the crews are overwhelmed.

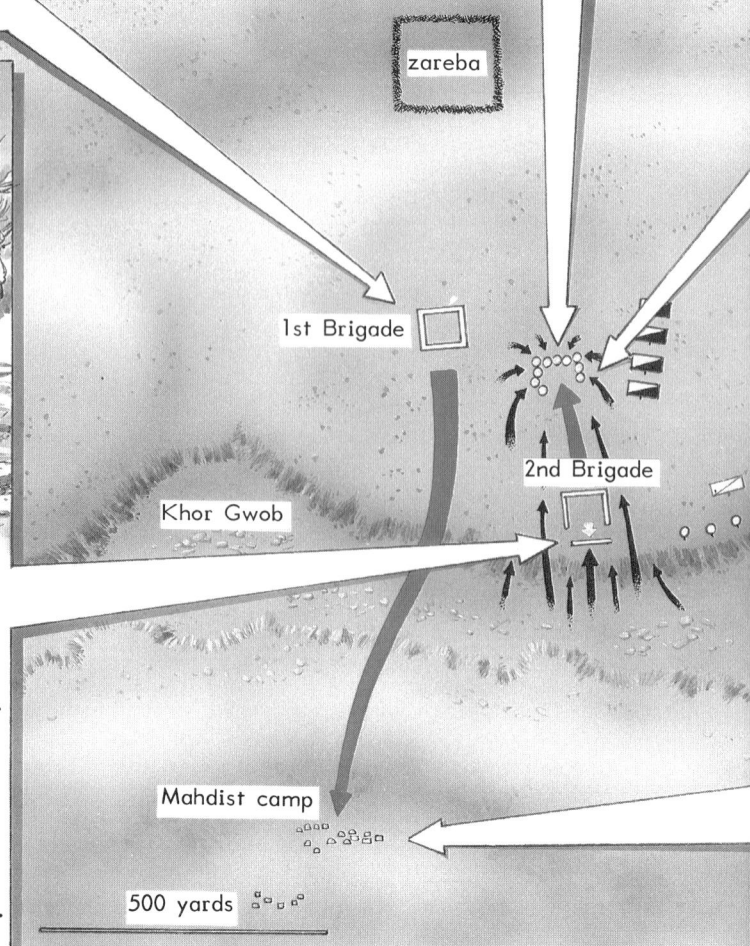

Battle in Africa

09.40 The remnants of the 2nd Brigade begin to rally, as
-10.00 Buller's firepower decimates the Mahdists thronging around the stricken square. Stewart's troopers circle to the left, dismount, and bring carbine fire to bear against the right flank of the Hadendowah. Caught between two fires, the enemy begins a slow fall-back.

10.15 The 1st Brigade continues to advance, pouring fire into the massed Hadendowah and preventing a fresh assault on Davis' men, who reform and rest.

10.30 The 2nd Brigade replenishes its ammunition and advances in line, recapturing the Gatlings and Gardners abandoned earlier.

11.00 The 2nd Brigade halts close to the ravine, facing the enemy on the far side. Graham orders the first Brigade to advance and drive the Hadendowah from the ridgeline, some 800 yards ahead. Clumps of Mahdist warriors are dispersed by artillery fire.

11.20 Buller's attack pushes into the Khor and then up the
-11.40 slopes. Disheartened, the enemy retires before him. From the crest Osman Digna's camp is revealed in the valley below: it is captured and burnt.

12.00 Squads of men seek out the British wounded. Others 'deal with' injured Arabs. The 2nd Brigade draws back to the Zareba while the cavalry pushes on to ensure that the enemy is in full retreat. Osman Digna, who had watched the action from the hilltop, has long disappeared. British losses are 91 killed, 110 wounded and 19 missing - 70 of the dead fell during the breaking of Davis' square. Mahdist losses are over 2,000 killed, from a force of 8-12,000 men. Of these 600 are counted on the site of the broken British square. No prisoners are taken.

Having looked at the battle of Tamai through British eyes, it is interesting to look at Osman Digna's own despatch: "... an English army of, it is said, 20,000 men including 6,000 horsemen arrived in the neighbourhood... the Ansar attacked them, and fought them the whole day until both forces retreated; the English returned to Suakin with a loss of 8,000 men."

European Battle Plans

Successful European battle plans, according to Callwell, were offensive - designed to 'impose battle' on the enemy. Plans would be simple, relying less on complex manoeuvres than upon maximising firepower while avoiding African ambushes or encirclements. Elaborate movements or timings usually went wrong, allowed the enemy to disappear or - worse - attack the Europeans in detail. It was found to be preferable to rely on a few basic well-tried tactics again and again:

1 Night March and Dawn Assault Irregular forces seldom kept proper camp security, and could be surprised by enemies whom - in daytime - had been perceived as slow and near-sighted.

2 Flank Attack Distracting the enemy's attention by a feint in front, then bringing a force onto his wings or rear.

3 Provoking Attack against a prepared firing line, using artillery harassment or small skirmish groups to irritate the foe until he makes a frontal charge into a fire trap.

Most European forces were fairly 'ad hoc' collections of units, lacking a habit of close co-operation with each other. Great flexibility and initiative were demanded of platoon or company commanders who found themselves in positions of local responsibility. Battlefield communications were basic and improvised, often with limited staff support. As the period progressed, infantry lines became thinner and more open - less prone to high casualties, but harder to control once the firing had started.

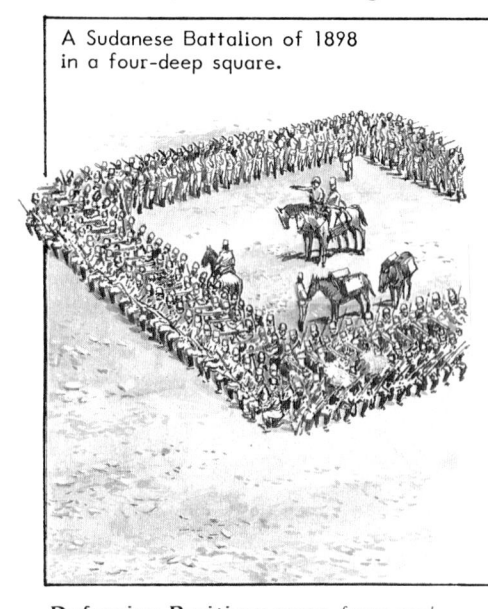

A Sudanese Battalion of 1898 in a four-deep square.

The Square was an archaic formation in European warfare, but found a new lease of life in the colonial arena. Against an enemy who sought to envelop flank and rear, and to charge with cold steel, the tightly-packed square was ideal. Its chief disadvantage was vulnerability to effective gunfire - but this was conspicuously lacking to Zulus, Moroccans and Mahdists.

Formed 2-4 ranks deep, with guns at the corners and baggage in the centre, the square was almost invulnerable for as long as morale and discipline held steady. It was also mobile, after a fashion. By advancing slowly (perhaps 25 yards per minute over good terrain), the square could force the foe to attack or fall back. Problems arose when gaps appeared in the ranks - especially at the corners - and care had to be taken to ensure that all parts of the square moved at the same speed. Often two mutually-supporting squares were employed: smaller squares were easier to control and if - as at Tamai - things went wrong, all was not totally lost.

Once the Africans attacked, a square would appear to be engulfed in assailants. At Bida (1897) 507 Hausa constables with six Maxims and seven guns fought two actions against the Emir of Nupe's 30,000 men, losing one officer and seven men for perhaps a thousand Fulani. In contrast, at El Teb, (1884) an Egyptian force of 3,500 men fell into complete confusion, and was almost annihilated when attacked by a Mahdist force only a quarter of its strength.

Defensive Positions were favoured if the Europeans felt they were at a disadvantage, or if the enemy was expected to launch an impetuous attack.

Defences could be linear or all-around: a natural line of suitable terrain could be used, as at Amba Alagi. Alternatively a site in open ground might be chosen in order to take full advantage of European firepower. The simplest defensive posture was to form up infantry and guns in line or square and await attack but, if time allowed, additional strength might be added by such things as trenches, breastworks and rifle pits, barricades of stores, sand- or mealie-bags, abatis, chevaux-de-frises, a thorn bush Zariba... or even kneeling camels. In Southern Africa the Boers formed their laagers from wagons arranged in square - and often dug into the earth.

Such works protected the troops from fire but also, more importantly, helped break the impetus of an African charge. At Rorke's Drift a company of the 24th Foot was able to hold off some 3-4,000 Zulus, thanks to their improvised fortification of the mission buildings and compound. In the final recourse, a mealie-bag redoubt served as an effective 'citadel' to repel the assault.

Boers defend a wagon laager.

Battle in Africa

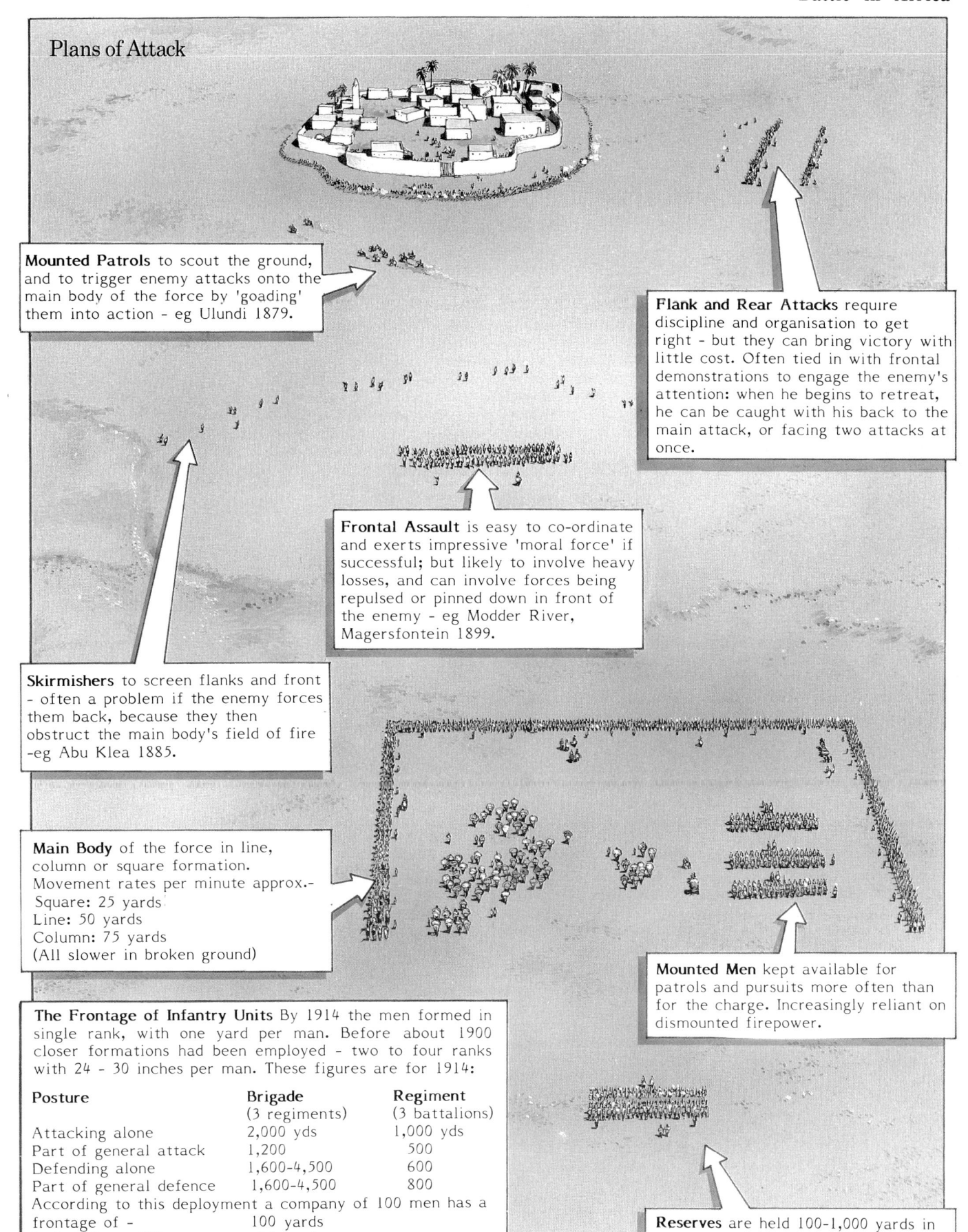

Plans of Attack

Mounted Patrols to scout the ground, and to trigger enemy attacks onto the main body of the force by 'goading' them into action - eg Ulundi 1879.

Flank and Rear Attacks require discipline and organisation to get right - but they can bring victory with little cost. Often tied in with frontal demonstrations to engage the enemy's attention: when he begins to retreat, he can be caught with his back to the main attack, or facing two attacks at once.

Frontal Assault is easy to co-ordinate and exerts impressive 'moral force' if successful; but likely to involve heavy losses, and can involve forces being repulsed or pinned down in front of the enemy - eg Modder River, Magersfontein 1899.

Skirmishers to screen flanks and front - often a problem if the enemy forces them back, because they then obstruct the main body's field of fire - eg Abu Klea 1885.

Main Body of the force in line, column or square formation. Movement rates per minute approx.-
Square: 25 yards
Line: 50 yards
Column: 75 yards
(All slower in broken ground)

Mounted Men kept available for patrols and pursuits more often than for the charge. Increasingly reliant on dismounted firepower.

The Frontage of Infantry Units By 1914 the men formed in single rank, with one yard per man. Before about 1900 closer formations had been employed - two to four ranks with 24 - 30 inches per man. These figures are for 1914:

Posture	Brigade (3 regiments)	Regiment (3 battalions)
Attacking alone	2,000 yds	1,000 yds
Part of general attack	1,200	500
Defending alone	1,600-4,500	600
Part of general defence	1,600-4,500	800

According to this deployment a company of 100 men has a frontage of - 100 yards
In 2 ranks at 30" per man - 42 yards
In 4 ranks at 30" per man - 21 yards

Reserves are held 100-1,000 yards in rear, to cover threats, bolster flagging units or fight rearguard actions.

African Battle Plans

African warfare had for centuries been based on limited principles - either raiding (for slaves or livestock), or formalised, consciously 'ceremonial' battles. In 1883, for example, a British traveller, Joseph Thompson, observed two Maasai armies, each some 3,000 strong, confronting each other to decide which of them should carry off their enemy's cattle. The outcome was determined not by a general clash of the two forces, but by a duel between selected detachments. There was thus an avoidance of 'real' warfare - for conquest and intimidation - since that would have been a far rougher game, which societies with limited manpower would not lightly have wished to play. Instead, African armies preferred to gain victory at the smallest cost, using the heroism of the 'mock battle' joined with the stealth and speed of the successful raid.

Real Battles, as opposed to 'mock battles', were sometimes undertaken. In this case envelopment was a usual object, the army advancing in a swift half-moon to assail the enemy's flanks and rear. Sudden attacks from natural cover might surprise and confuse an enemy, or the imposing spectacle of ceremonial warfare might be harnessed to give psychological superiority. In 1890 Carl Weise observed of Mpezeni's Ngoni army "... they try to intimidate the enemy by striking their shields, by the noises of bells attached to their skin clothing, and by strident shouts." This 'moral imperative' was usually linked to aggressive offensives - the massed charge of Fulani or Mahdist host was intended to break the will of its target before crashing into the demoralised foe. By combining impetuous resolution and sudden appearances, these tactics were ideally suited to brave but largely undisciplined warrior bands. They utilised the natural skills of the African fighting man - stealth, courage and mobility - to overcome the foe and crush him before he had time to react. Then the remnants could be pursued and cut down, and their livestock and wives plundered.

Control by chiefs was largely unnecessary, which was fortunate since it was almost impossible to apply once action had been joined. Their role lay more in deciding the initial direction and timing of the offensive. They rarely used defensive methods in open battle: if they did choose to stand their ground they would usually employ fortifications to increase their chances - bush Zarebas or Bomas, timber stockades or earthworks. In open battle, defensive tactics depended rather on fierce counter-attacks, as the enemy' assault lost cohesion - eg Shaka's defence at Gqokli Hill, 1818 - or on the use of chosen ground for concealment, as we have seen at Tamai.

Effective firearms modified these traditional tactics somewhat, by making assaults more difficult and more costly. Some African leaders, such as the Fulani Emirs, proved hidebound when confronted by this development. Others adapted successfully to new conditions and gave the European invader serious problems.

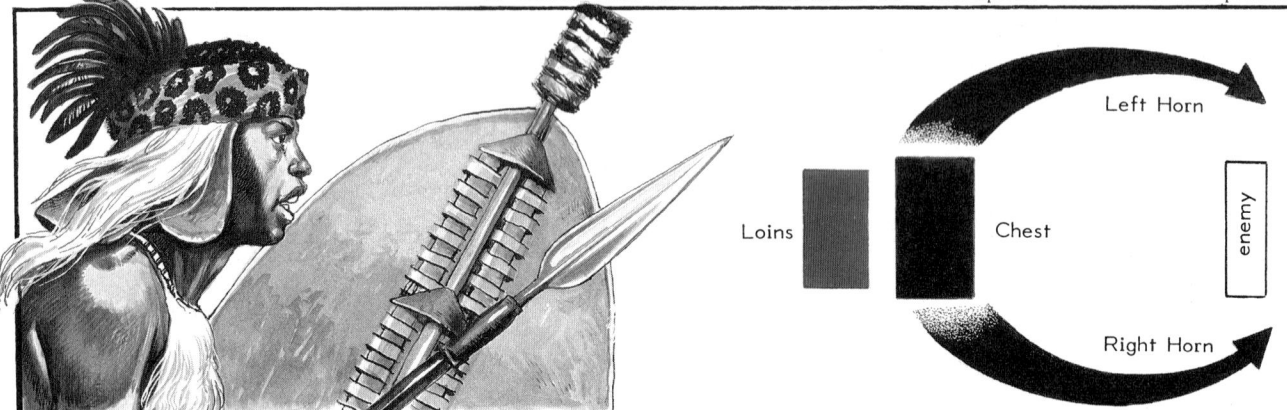

Maasai 'Moran' in full regalia.

Zulu warfare, based on the regimental system, represented the highest point of traditional African methods of fighting. Under Shaka the virtues of drill and organisation had been added to those of courage and speed. The envelopment tactics used by other Bantu peoples were refined by placing agile young regiments in the 'horns' of an impi, veteran warriors in the 'chest', and by adding a reserve in the rear - the 'loins'. The reserve would hold back from the action, sometimes even sitting with its back to the enemy, until called in for a decisive stroke. Every man knew his place precisely, and the resulting disciplined assault proved unstoppable by traditional enemies.

Zulu weapons were the fearsome broad-bladed stabbing spear, the "Iklwa" and the Knobkerrie. By the 1870s thousands of Zulus had aquired firearms, often as payment for working for Europeans or - after the victory at Isandhlwana - as battle booty. Command was in the hands of Indunas - experienced warriors who scouted the ground carefully before combat and directed the course of the action from a chosen vantage point. In 1879 Cetshwayo's army had some 55,000 men in 33 regiments, of which some 40,000 were available to fight. Other peoples also adopted Zulu methods - eg the Ndebele had perhaps 20,000 warriors in 1893, composed of the Zansi (descendents of Mzilikazi's Zulu emigrants), the Enhla ('those from along the way') and the Holi (absorbed Shona tribesmen). The Ngoni incursions also brought Zulu methods into East and central Africa, where the Hehe and others adopted them.

Battle in Africa

Tuareg warfare epitomised the fighting style of all the desert nomads. In 1860 a Frenchman, Henri Duveyrier wrote that "To see a Tuareg war charge is to feel complete and utter fear creep through one's body. Great serried squadrons of tall, blue-veiled men, mounted on fast white camels crashing forward like a vast roller."

In 1896 a French military explorer, Lt. Hourst, visited the Tuareg and wrote of their raiding. In these secret operations less than 100 men, chosen for their skills, might go "gliding silently between the encampments of the enemy..." If the subjects of the raid were alerted, their men would flee but the women remain: "No Tuareg would stain his hands with the blood of a defenceless woman."

Hourst echoed Duveyrier in his account of a battle. Tradition was the key, with strict forms of ritual. It was "like a set of quadrilles... a medieval tournament". So traditional was Tuareg battle that at Izewan (1898) the Kel Dennik warriors demanded that the Kel Ahaggar - Northern Tuareg from Algeria - lay down their guns and fight with sword and spear (sensibly the Ahaggar refused). Battle began with hurled insults, and the throwing of spears, and a rush "stabbing at each other with their daggers, or trying to crack each other's skulls with their stone amulets..." Personal combat between chiefs was common. Hourst felt that fighting on foot was more usual than mounted, but this may have been because the 'lower orders' - the negro Bouzous and the Blacksmith class - had no horses. Tuareg nobles preferred to ride, using horses on the southern savannahs, camels in the desert.

Boer tactics traditionally relied upon the mobility of their ponies and the firepower of their expert marksmen. In the 1830s and '40s Boer commandos had defeated the Ndebele and Zulus by provoking their warriors, by stinging attacks with mounted riflemen, into assaulting a wagon-laager. The Afrikaners could then shoot down the charging enemy from a secure position, while their wives and children reloaded the weapons. Against the more sophisticated and cautious British the advantage of mobility was emphasised still further, at a strategic level. Battle plans, however, tended to be defensive, relying on concealed single guns and carefully hidden trenches. At Modder River the Boers lined the river bank, while at Magersfontein the innovative Koos de la Rey chose to dig trenches at the base of a line of hills. Lord Methuen bombarded the hilltops, and hit nobody.

Defensive methods suited the independent Afrikaner citizen-soldiers very well. Without the organisation needed to handle complex manoeuvres and with an inordinate fear of flank or rear attacks, the major Boer armies of 1899 were at their best in static sharpshooting. More cohesive small units, however, had a greater range of choices. Select bands like the volunteers who stormed Majuba Hill, the "Zarps" of the Johannesburg police, or the fierce 'Bitter Ender' Commandos of 1900-2, could assault British positions in rushes covered by their comrades. The guerillas also revised the cavalry charge, by galloping at the enemy in an open order line, firing rapidly from the saddle and enveloping the flanks. High morale and tight unit control were the essence of this late-war raiding.

Boer Shelter-trench. The Boers made extensive use of fieldworks which varied in type from the elaborate style shown here, to shallow scrapes in the ground.

Ambushes and night attacks. The element of surprise was a vital ingredient in African warfare. It was doubly valuable in resisting the Europeans, since fieldcraft, mobility and local knowledge were their weakest suit. And if the white men could be caught unawares, his frightening technical strength and organisational resilience might be overcome. Night approaches were one way to attack the Europeans. At Intombi Drift in 1879 a Zulu impi took advantage of early morning mist to come within 50 yards of Captain Moriarty's laager. They fired a volley, threw down their guns and rushed. "So quickly did they come", wrote an officer, "there was really no defence on the part of our men... in a very few minutes all was over, our men simply slaughtered". At Menhaba (April 1908) 5,000 Moroccans attacked two Foreign Legion companies in camp under cover of darkness. A series of bayonet charges finally cleared the bivouac, but only after 120 legionnaires had fallen. The Moroccans made off with rifles, mules and stores.

In daylight hours the Africans turned to the use of natural cover. At Dul Madoba in 1913 Yusuf's Somalis were able to use thorn brush - which cut visibility to 100-400 yards - to approach and defeat Captain Corfield's Camel Constabulary. At Shaykan (1883) Wad-el-Nejumi hid Jehadia riflemen in the treetops to fire against Hicks Pasha's squares. In March 1905 an impetuous German officer, Major Glasenapp, led 56 officers and men straight into a Herero ambush at Owikokorero: entering a clearing, the Germans were caught in column by heavy fire. In 30 minutes 26 men were killed before Glasenapp was able to retreat.

African Leadership

Leadership was an essential factor in African resistance to the European invader. In societies where there were few established structures of power, or where authority was imbued with religious significance, a dynamic leader was necessary to focus the efforts of the people. Where leadership was aggressive and charismatic, the colonial advance could be slowed and even beaten back. Where weak or unpopular leaders were in charge, resistance was likely to be disorganised or disputed. The military power of the Zulus and Ndebele was hardly reflected in their indecisive leadership, and the Fulani states proved very brittle in face of the British approach. By contrast a determined leader could oppose the colonial advance to a degree far beyond his apparent military strength. Lat Dior, the Damel of Cayor in Senegal, was able to resist the French for no less than five years before he was killed in 1886.

Successful African leaders tended to be flexible in their strategies, modernisers of their weaponry and methods, and - most important of all - survivors. A dogged and subtle leader could often prolong his campaign for years, whereas the sudden demise of a leader was usually a signal to his army to disperse as a routed rabble.

Dynamism was the crucial element in African leadership - the key ingredient that made all the difference between a sustained resistance and early collapse. In Senegal Lat Dior expressed this in no uncertain terms: 'as long as I live, be well assured, I shall oppose with all my might the construction of this railway... even were I to go to rest, my horse 'Malay' would give you the same answer'.

Personal energy could express itself in overtly 'heroic' leadership, such as the chivalrous Wad El Nejumi leading his men to victory at Shaykan (1883) and Khartoum (1885), and then to destruction at Toski (1889). Others, like Samori and Rabeh of Sennar, built empires by the force of arms. Most characteristic of Africa at this period were those who simply survived, against great odds, to fight again. Hendrik Witbooi (1838-1905) led a small Hottentot band into the Kalahari in 1904-5 to renew a guerrilla war against the Germans that had ended ten years earlier. Mkwawa, victor of Lugalo in 1891, held out until 1898, living as a fugitive for four years until he shot himself rather than be taken. It was the resolution of the professional survivors - Bou Amana in Algeria, Osman Digna in the Sudan, De Wet and Smuts in South Africa - which did most to ensure the European conquest was such a long drawn-out affair.

Mahdist Emirs in discussion before Omdurman.

Case Study 1 - Decision Making
The Khalifa Before Omdurman, September 1898

In theory the Khalifa Abdullahi was a divinely inspired autocrat, appointed by the Mahdi of God. In practice his decisions were reached by consultation with groups of warrior emirs and other leading men. Councils were held on August 31st and in the afternoon and evening of September 1st, to determine a policy in the face of Kitchener's army. The Khalifa's lieutenants argued the pros and cons of each option in turn:

OPTION	ADVANTAGES	DISADVANTAGES	RESULT
1 Abandon Omdurman, retire to the Kordofan deserts to wage guerilla warfare.	Uses techniques successful in 1881-5; stretches enemy supply lines.	Means abandoning the capital - and the Mahdi's sacred tomb.	Not chosen - the proposer thrown into jail!
2 Use the city of Omdurman as a defensive position.	Uses protection of fortifications.	Negate's army's offensive spirit; endangers civilians.	Not chosen, partly because of recent enemy shelling.
3 Make a night attack on Kitchener's position.	Negates Kitchener's massive firepower.	Loss of control, and of firepower.	Not chosen.
4 Make a daylight attack on Kitchener's position.	Maximises Mahdist rifle fire and evokes the Mahdi's vision of a victory outside Omdurman.	Allows enemy firepower its full effect.	Chosen - with disastrous consequences.

Ibrahim Al Khalil, a leading warrior, had argued for a night attack, but had been opposed by the Khalifa's son and heir, Sheik Al Din. Finally the Khalifa followed his son's proposal of a daylight battle for the political reason that it offered the best confirmation of the Mahdi's vision, and hence of himself and his heir as true successors of the Mahdi.

Battle in Africa

The Origins of successful African leaders were frequently similar. Most began life as sons of moderate-to-important local families; received better than usual educations, and showed 'promise' during their youth. El Raisuni (c 1870-1925) was a Koranic scholar and lawyer who became a major bandit Caid in the Rif mountains of Morocco. Using education, cunning and the prestige of descent from an important Moroccan saint, Raisuni's career encompassed jails and palaces in a chequered path that for one brief moment even made him Caid of Tangiers. Menelik of Shoa was a significant regional ruler in the 1870s, before accepting Italian cash and arms to act as a counterweight to the Emperor Yohannis. He was thus able to extend his personal power to the lowlands south of Shoa, and force Yohannis to recognise him as successor. On his succession in 1889 he turned on the Italians, lured their allies into his camp and massively defeated them (1895-6), uniting Ethiopia under his rule.

African leaders born to positions of great authority often had to fight for their inheritance. Cetshwayo defeated a rival to the Zulu throne in 1856, while Lobengula had to crush dissent before he could succeed Mzilikazi at the head of the Ndebele. Thus African leaders were often the best qualified of their peer groups to attain positions of power.

Louis Botha encourages his men under fire at Spion Kop

The Death of a Leader was likely to mean the dissolution of his army. Yohannis of Ethiopia was killed at the moment of victory at Gallabat (1889), and his forces collapsed into a rabble. Mamadou Lamine survived a shell that blew up his HQ as his warriors stormed the city of Bakel (1886) - but he was unable to halt the resulting rout. The personal charisma that held many African armies together was a poor substitute for the more lasting regular discipline and organisation that they lacked.

Case Study 2 - Command in Action
Boer Leadership at Spion Kop, January 1899

The British seizure of the key Tugela position of Spion Kop during the night of 23rd January was reported to Louis Botha, the Boer leader, at 5 am on the 24th. His options were:
1 To hold what remained of the Tugela line position.
2 To withdraw from the Tugela.
3 To counter-attack immediately.
4 To organise a counter-attack later.
5 Wire to Pretoria for new orders.

In the event he chose to counter-attack immediately, even if it would be piecemeal, gambling that a bold initiative could repulse the British on the hill before they could dig in or be significantly reinforced.

The Sequence of Events:
5 am to Noon -
- Botha calls commandants Daniel Opperman (Pretoria Commando) and Hendrik Prinsloo (Carolina Commando) to tell them to lead an assault on the kop.
- Botha sends messages to artillery commanders to fire on the summit of the kop.
- He rides from laager to laager, reassuring the men and selecting some 1,000 (out of 4,000) to attack the invader.
- He informs co-commander Schalk Burger that all is under control.
- He informs Pretoria of events, by telegram.

Noon to Midnight -
- Botha monitors the progress of the battle - a protracted bloodbath with heavy losses.
- He encourages the men to continue, when morale threatens to break down, but Burger retires at 5 pm and Opperman at 10 pm. Battle dies out.
- Botha watches for other British moves against the now dangerously-spread Boer line.

Midnight to dawn
- Botha rallies his men by riding from laager to laager all night. Partial success.
- 3 am Receives report that British are retreating from the summit.
- Boers advance to the summit and find it abandoned.
- Daylight c 4.30 am: British retreat is confirmed. Victory seized from the jaws of defeat!

31

The New Technology

From the middle of the nineteenth century, the rate of technological progress accelerated sharply. In the field of weaponry these advances meant that to be a few years behind the times was to be at a considerable disadvantage - but it also meant that conservative military establishments often failed to exploit fully the most recent developments.

The Breech-loading rifle was standard equipment for European troops by 1879. These were advanced 'second generation' weapons developed from the converted muzzle-loaders of the previous decade. They were capable of rapid fire at ranges far beyond those previously known - eg the British Martini-Henry M1871 was sighted to 1,450 yards and could fire a heavy bullet every five seconds, while even its carbine variant was sighted to 1,180 yards. Comparable weapons were used by the continental armies - the German M1871 Mauser, the French Le Gras of 1874 and the Italian M1870 Vetterli. Older weapons were sold or passed on; Egypt equipped its infantry with American Remington rolling block rifles, while the Indian army received British Sniders as the Redcoats took up the Martini.

In tests the new rifles proved enormously accurate - and in the right hands they could be in combat, too. In 1895 a Scots trader, Andrew Dick, and two French companions shot and killed 100 Maasai warriors before they were overwhelmed. In general terms, however, the new weapons were far less effective in the field than their makers had hoped. There were some technical problems - eg the Martini kicked like a mule, fouled easily, and suffered from spent cartridges jamming in the breech when, in the heat of battle their brass Boxer casings expanded too much. More importantly, the troops were woefully ill-trained to deal with sophisticated weaponry. At Gingindhlovu the scout John Dunn observed that when the Zulus came within 300 yards the British regulars "still had the long-range sights up", and that they were "firing wildly in any direction". Moreover the smoke of the black powder weapons meant that a thick fog quickly enveloped the firing line. Officers preferred volley fire to the - theoretically more accurate - 'Independent Fire' simply because volleys gave the smoke a chance to lift. Volleys also allowed a much greater degree of fire discipline. In the excitement of battle soldiers would begin to fire uncontrollably, which with the rapid fire of modern weapons meant that a unit could quite easily expend all its ammunition before order could be restored. At Omdurman, in Macdonald's Sudanese brigade, the officers resorted to issuing cartridges three at a time, to preserve ammunition, but still could not control their soldiers. Thus it was far more sensible to hold fire until the enemy was 7-900 yards away, then maintain steady, slow volleys, than to explore the long range limits of the weapon. Although Count Gleichen records cases when picked marksmen hit their man at 1,800 yards, most regulars could not expect to hit a target beyond 450 yards.

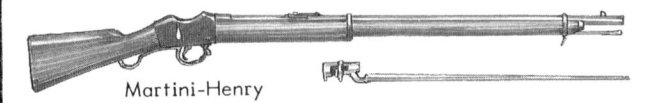

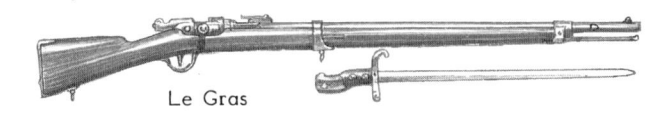

Martini-Henry

Le Gras

The magazine rifle. In 1884 the Germans converted their Mauser breech-loader to an eight-cartridge magazine. Other nations followed: the French Lebel was introduced in 1886, the Italian Vetterli was converted to a four-round repeater in 1887 and the British Lee-Metford, with an eight-round magazine was authorised in 1888 (Increased to 10 rounds in 1892.) These new rifles were small-bore weapons, .315" for the Lebel, .303" for the Lee Metford, which meant lighter, easier-to-carry ammunition. They could fire up to 3,000 yards (the 1898 Mauser was sighted to 2,200 yards), and could maintain even faster rates of fire. However the real advance, for military purposes, was the appearance of the smokeless propellant Cordite in 1892. Firing lines were no longer wreathed in thick white smoke and, while no officer would ever consider allowing his men to fire 20-30 rounds per minute (10-12 was the fastest at which discipline could be maintained), the Magazine certainly allowed greater flexibility, especially in the attack. The surprise for many was the discovery that smokeless ammunition kept a concealed adversary hidden - a fact that was perceived by the Boers and other irregulars before it was by their regular foes.

Gatling gun manned by sailors at Alexandria 1882.

The machine gun in 1879 was no longer either an amusing novelty or, as it had been in the Franco-Prussian War, a 'secret weapon'. The Gatling company made a variety of hand-operated guns available on field carriages, naval mountings and even - as a promotional stunt - mounted on a camel saddle. British naval Gatlings had ten barrels and could fire, in theory, 600 rounds per minute, but were so seriously prone to jamming that the actual rate was nearer 280. In 1874 a Gardner model was introduced which fired 120 rounds per minute per barrel (guns were made with one, two or five barrels). Later a Nordenfeldt gun appeared which exceeded the Gatling's rate of fire and was free from its technical problems. But the real advance came with the Maxim - a water-cooled gun operated by its own recoil. Vastly more reliable than previous models, the Maxim had comparable range (1,000 yards) but twice the rate of fire: 1,100-1,200 rounds per minute. It was adopted by the British army in 1891 and soon became the key enforcer of British rule in many parts of Africa. Weighing only 60 pounds, it was therefore sufficiently portable to overawe even the most inaccessible and intransigent headmen. In 1887 an exhibition of its fire left the Yonni of Sierra Leone 'deeply impressed'.

Battle in Africa

Artillery used in Africa ranged from light, portable mountain guns to enormous naval pieces capable of sending 50lb shells several miles. During the period 1879-1914 the development of ordnance saw major improvements, such as reliable breech loading, smokeless powder, new and powerful explosives - the French Melinite and the British Lyddite. There were also quick-firing (QF) guns like the French M1897 75mm cannon, which could fire 20-30 rounds per minute. The 37mm Pom Pom - a tiny QF gun - fired a 1lb shell every two seconds. A survey of the 1899 British Rifled Breech Loading (RBL) equipment which replaced the Rifled Muzzle Loaders (RML) of the 1880s gives us some ranges:
12pdr RBL - 3,800 yards with shrapnel
15pdr RBL - 4,100 yards with shrapnel
(Both the above ranges were increased by 1,800 yards when better fuses were introduced around 1900.)
4.7" QF naval gun - 10,000 yards with HE or shrapnel
5" howitzer (50lb Lyddite shell) - 4,800 yards

A British artillery battery at regulation intervals. 20 yards was allowed between guns. Where incoming artillery fire was expected on the battery position, the ammunition wagons would be further in the rear, or in cover.

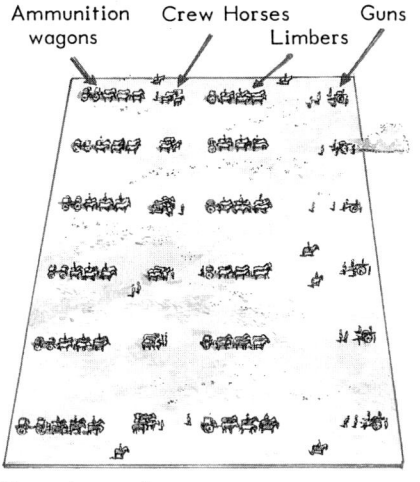

Ammunition wagons — Crew — Horses — Limbers — Guns

It was the small 'mountain' gun that proved most useful in Africa. The 1877 2.5" RML weighed 400lbs, broke down into five loads for mules, camels or a train of porters - and could fire shrapnel 3,300 yards, or common shell 4,000 (with case shot as a close-range standby). Incredibly versatile, this 7 pdr piece proved invaluable in bush warfare until the Boer War demonstrated that short range, black powder weapons were outmoded. In 1903 a 10 pdr RBL model with a range of 6,000 yards was introduced. At the same period the recoil mechanisms pioneered by Creusot and Krupps became standardised, and protective shields were added to field guns.

The British made some use of William Hale's rockets - steel tubes of explosive fired from a 'trough'. They had a range of more than a mile but were erratic in flight. Some were successful in frightening Fode Silla's men in the Gambia (1894), but their use was not widespread.

The Africans get firearms. Before the arrival of Europeans, African weapons had consisted of spears - from light javelins to huge, leaf-blades - bows, axes, clubs, knives and swords. Firearms, traded for slaves, made some people very powerful. Yet although certain chiefs could field thousands of gunmen - one Nyamwezi headman had 20,000 in 1883 - most were archaic. Inlaid Berber muskets and West African 'Dane guns' were joined by a vast influx of old European muskets, especially the Tower 'Brown Bess'. Realising that these weapons could not compare with modern rifles, several African leaders sought out contacts who could give them something better. Menelik acquired 25,000 rifles between 1882 and 1887, and many more from Russian and French agents in the 1890s: before Adowa he had over 80,000 modern rifles - Martini, Gras, Lebel and Remington models - some of them supplied by the Italians themselves. In West Africa Samori Toure developed his armed strength by careful study of new weapons. From 1876 to 1885 he used French Chassepots, then replaced them with Gras rifles and the Kropatschek repeater - his blacksmiths could make excellent replicas of these. From 1888 he began to acquire magazine rifles, and had 6,000 by 1893. He even managed to infiltrate spies into French munitions factories in Senegal, to learn new methods of manufacture.

In 1890 the European powers agreed to stop selling modern arms to Africans. This was only partially successful, but did at least ensure that heavy weapons stayed out of African hands. Samori could never acquire artillery, while the Mahdists, who had a good deal of captured Egyptian equipment, lacked ammunition and skilled gunners. Only the Boers - who were as much European as they were African - were able to buy whatever they chose. The Transvaal government purchased some 70 artillery pieces: 75mm and 155mm Creusots from France, 120mm Krupp Howitzers from Germany, and 37mm Vickers-Maxim QF guns - the famous Pom Poms - from their soon-to-be adversaries in England.

The Remington Rolling-block rifle, shown above, and in detail with the breech open, fell into the hands of the Mahdists in large numbers after the defeat of Hicks' column in 1883.

The Power of Fire

The cutting edge of European attacks, and the salvation of European defensive lines, could often be found in European firepower. Using 'the new technology', a small body of troops now at last had an excellent chance of defeating very greatly superior numbers of enemy at ranges up to 1,000 yards. If the Europeans could mass their fire sufficiently at the key point - and maintain adequate supplies of ammunition - they could usually manage to hold their ground while inflicting very heavy casualties.

The African Use of Firearms varied. Moroccan horsemen had been using matchlock and flintlock muskets - often beautifully crafted weapons - for three centuries in an impressive but largely ineffective style. Riders would approach the enemy, halt, fire a shot, then retire to reload in best 16th century manner - a tactic much appreciated by their opponents armed with breechloaders. For most Africans firearms were a recent innovation, useful in slave-raiding or elephant hunting, but causing few changes in traditional tactics. The Zulus used rifles largely to cover the attack of their impis, but were completely unable to contest the British fire superiority (eg at Kambula, when they had captured modern weapons but found them strange and mysterious items). Ndebele warriors believed that by pushing the sights as far forward as possible they would make the bullet strike home harder. Mahdists often shortened the barrels of their Remington rifles to make them easier to carry. There was no real appreciation of the Europeans' overwhelming superiority in training, and at Omdurman the Mahdists were confident that their riflemen would be a match for Kitchener's.

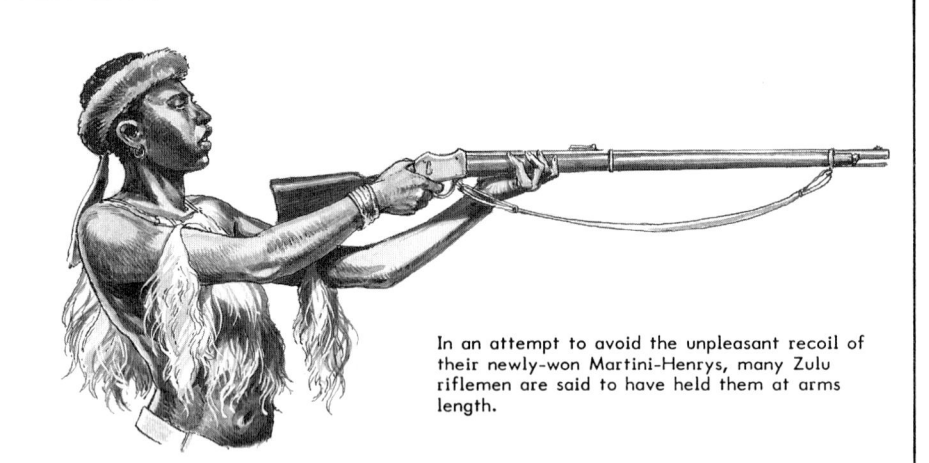

The Ethiopians used modern rifles as assault weapons, firing as their massed formations closed for combat. In contrast to this, there were some peoples who made an effective combination of traditional fieldcraft skills with modern firepower. The German Official History maintained that the Hottentots and Herero were more dangerous foes than the Boers, because of their sniping from cover. Equally in Somalia the Mullah's forces employed an efficient 'fire and movement' system of short rushes in extended order, making careful use of brush cover.

In an attempt to avoid the unpleasant recoil of their newly-won Martini-Henrys, many Zulu riflemen are said to have held them at arms length.

Artillery Doctrine was forged from a combination of theory and experience. There was general agreement on the main points:-
1 Guns should be pushed forward to inflict maximum casualties and achieve maximum 'morale effect'.
2 Bombardments should not be used if they will cause the enemy to withdraw, since the object is to defeat him rather than to drive him away.
3 If a bombardment is used, enemy guns should be silenced before firing on the section of line to be attacked. Guns were placed at intervals of 12 - 20 yards, usually in the open with teams and vehicles under cover in the rear. The Boer War showed the problems with this directive: at Colenso Col Long pushed his guns to within 700 yards of the Boer line, and watched his crews mown down. Long ranges and smokeless powder also meant that targets could not always be seen or identified. At Talana and Stormberg the British gunners bombarded their own infantry: at Colenso and Spion Kop they refrained from shelling Boers whom they took to be fellow Britons.

British artillery engaging the enemy under rifle fire at Colenso. Note the distance between guns.

Royal Artillery Equipment, Egypt 1882
Per Battery
6 guns & limbers
6 ammunition wagons
1 store wagon
1 store limber wagon
1 forage wagon
1 water cart
1 cavalry spring cart

Ammunition
i) With the battery

	per battery		Per gun	
	13 pdr	16	13 pdr	16
Common shell	180	144	30	24
Shrapnel	648	432	108	72
Case shot	24	24	4	4
Star shells	800	800	133	133

ii) In Ordnance Department stores

Common shell	2000	288	333	48
Shrapnel	720	864	120	144
Case shot	28	48	46	8

Battle in Africa

Infantry Firepower: an 'ideal' situation, where a massed attack in the open is met by fresh, steady European troops:

Company of 100 men

African warriors moving 100 yards per minute

At extreme range the Martini-Henry is sighted using the very top of the extended rear sight. If there was time, range markers were placed in front of the unit.

LONG RANGE: 700 - 1,400 yards
7 minutes' fire at 6 shots per minute, 2% effectiveness = 84 casualties.

Visibility distances 'with good eyesight':-
1,700 yards - masses of troops can be recognised
1,300 yards - infantry can be distinguished from cavalry
1,000 yards - individuals may be seen
700 yards - head, crossbelts &c can be distinguished
500 yards - uniforms recognised, weapons visible 'if bright'
250 yards - officers recognisable from men, uniform clear

- from 'The Artillerist's Manual', a mid-Victorian work. Recent developments in optical equipment gave officers 6 - 8 times magnification with binoculars, or much more with portable naval telescopes.

Beyond visibility ranges, dust could be seen: a thick cloud indicates infantry, a high thin cloud indicates mounted men, a broken cloud artillery or wagons.

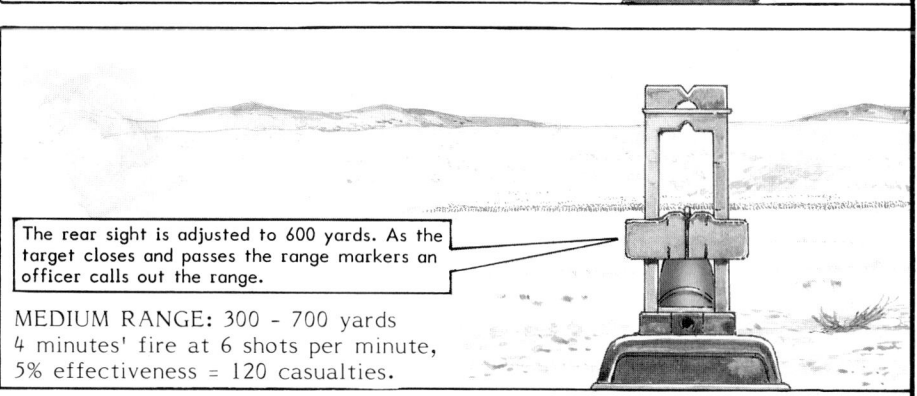

The rear sight is adjusted to 600 yards. As the target closes and passes the range markers an officer calls out the range.

MEDIUM RANGE: 300 - 700 yards
4 minutes' fire at 6 shots per minute, 5% effectiveness = 120 casualties.

Warriors begin to run: 150 yards per minute.

Bayonet fixed

CLOSE RANGE: 100 - 300 yards
2 minutes' fire at 6 shots per minute, at 10% effectiveness = 120 casualties.

Warriors charge: 200 yards per minute.

At close range the rear sight is lowered. It was almost impossible to maintain disciplined volley fire at close quarters and the men would fire as quickly as they could. In the circumstances shown here, it is extremely unlikely that the charge would have got this close!

POINT BLANK: 0 - 100 yards
30 seconds at 10 shots per minute, 15% effectiveness = 75 casualties.

Overall casualties = 399 in 12½ minutes' firing, 83 rounds per man, or 13 more than normally carried on the person. This shows the need for careful conservation of fire.

Note that although casualties per shot are low, the overall effect is enough to disable four times the number of those firing. At Omdurman 200,000 bullets and 1,000 shells hit 12,000 Mahdists at long and medium range. This total would have been reduced if visibility had been less good or the target concealed/in open order, or the troops fatigued: eg. at Jidbali in Somalia (1904) it needed 600 rounds per hit.

The Volume of Fire was as important as the casualties inflicted, in deterring the enemy assault. A company in traditional close order two deep would have a frontage of 40 yards: at 600 shots per minute a volume of 15 shots per yard per minute could be maintained - enough to subdue the fiercest attack.

Cold Steel - the climax of battle

'Cold Steel' - the cherished myth of the bayonet thrust and the sabre slash - gained a new lease of life in the African wars. Infantry assaults with naked bayonets - increasingly difficult against modern opponents - were invaluable against a foe who was unable to inflict serious casualties by fire. The bayonet charge combined two of the Europeans' greatest assets: discipline and aggressive spirit. It was easy to prepare and control - far easier than lengthy firefights which often tailed off into wasteful, ineffective skirmishing. It confirmed a moral superiority over the recipients and - most of all - it was decisive. The victims might not lose as many men as they would by, say, making a charge against a square's musketry; but they would know they had been roundly beaten - and would be unlikely to venture into combat again!

Many African peoples relied heavily on shock tactics, and relished hand-to-hand combat. The Tuareg held ornate weaponry - iron lances and swords - in great esteem. The new Zulu warfare of Shaka had focussed upon the broad-headed stabbing assegai, and provided a moral impetus that broke traditional Bantu foes. In contrast, fighters without mêlée weapons were loth to engage closely. Fode Sila's men refused to face the charge of the West Indian Regiment in 1894, while the Boers considered shock weapons 'brutal and unchristian': after the pursuit at Elandslaagte they threatened to shoot any lancers they captured. Few Boers would face a bayonet charge, preferring to run or surrender; and fewer still would use assault tactics. Only the very best commandos - the "Zarps", the foreign volunteers and the Bitter-Enders - were able to launch effective storm assaults, which included their own magazine rifle fire.

In Africa, as in Europe, the climax of most successful bayonet assaults was the arrival of the attacking force in the hastily deserted position of the enemy.

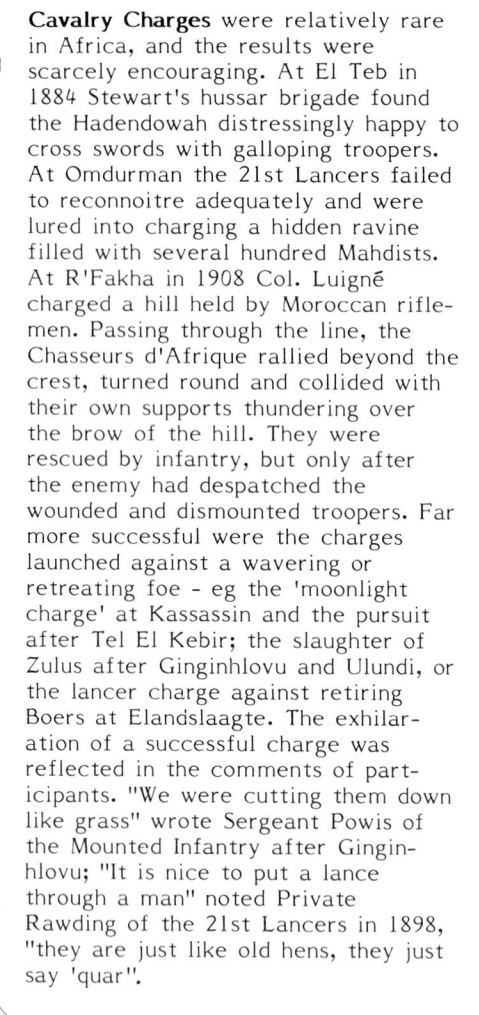

Cavalry Charges were relatively rare in Africa, and the results were scarcely encouraging. At El Teb in 1884 Stewart's hussar brigade found the Hadendowah distressingly happy to cross swords with galloping troopers. At Omdurman the 21st Lancers failed to reconnoitre adequately and were lured into charging a hidden ravine filled with several hundred Mahdists. At R'Fakha in 1908 Col. Luigné charged a hill held by Moroccan riflemen. Passing through the line, the Chasseurs d'Afrique rallied beyond the crest, turned round and collided with their own supports thundering over the brow of the hill. They were rescued by infantry, but only after the enemy had despatched the wounded and dismounted troopers. Far more successful were the charges launched against a wavering or retreating foe - eg the 'moonlight charge' at Kassassin and the pursuit after Tel El Kebir; the slaughter of Zulus after Ginginhlovu and Ulundi, or the lancer charge against retiring Boers at Elandslaagte. The exhilaration of a successful charge was reflected in the comments of participants. "We were cutting them down like grass" wrote Sergeant Powis of the Mounted Infantry after Ginginhlovu; "It is nice to put a lance through a man" noted Private Rawding of the 21st Lancers in 1898, "they are just like old hens, they just say 'quar'".

The Crisis of Battle was rarely preceded by long preparatory artillery duels or skirmishing. There might be a long period of quiet, followed by a short and bloody clash at close range. African attacks often brewed up quickly, emerging as a charge from cover, rather than the slow manoeuvres of regular armies. Thus at Abu Kru in 1885 the British took 3½ - 4 hours to prepare their attack, under constant harassing fire, then there was a ten-minute sequence of advance, fierce Mahdist charge, and victory won by the massive firepower of the regulars. Other battles in which 'shock-oriented' African peoples attacked the Europeans showed a similar profile of long-but-crucial quiet spells punctuated by brief, frenetic crises. Examples are Ulundi, Omdurman, Bou Othmann. By contrast the Boer battles displayed a more 'European' and 'technical' sequence: artillery bombardments lasting for hours or even days, then cumbrous infantry assaults either cleared Boer positions at heavy cost or, more often, bogged down at 1,000 - 1,200 yards from the line. The stalled attackers would lie on their stomachs in the sun, awaiting the fall of night or an initiative from HQ that would enable them to regroup, refill bellies and canteens, and regain their offensive spirit.

36

Battle in Africa

Cavalry Late Victorian theory emphasised that cavalry was for scouting, pursuit and dismounted firepower; but the cavalrymen themselves preferred to think in terms of the 'arme blanche' and the traditional knee-to-knee mounted charge. The basic precepts of the charge had changed little in a century, as follows:-

Cavalry Speeds were kept slow, to help maintain control and order.
The Walk: 60-80 yards per minute
The Trot: 120-160 " " "
The Gallop: 180-240 " " "

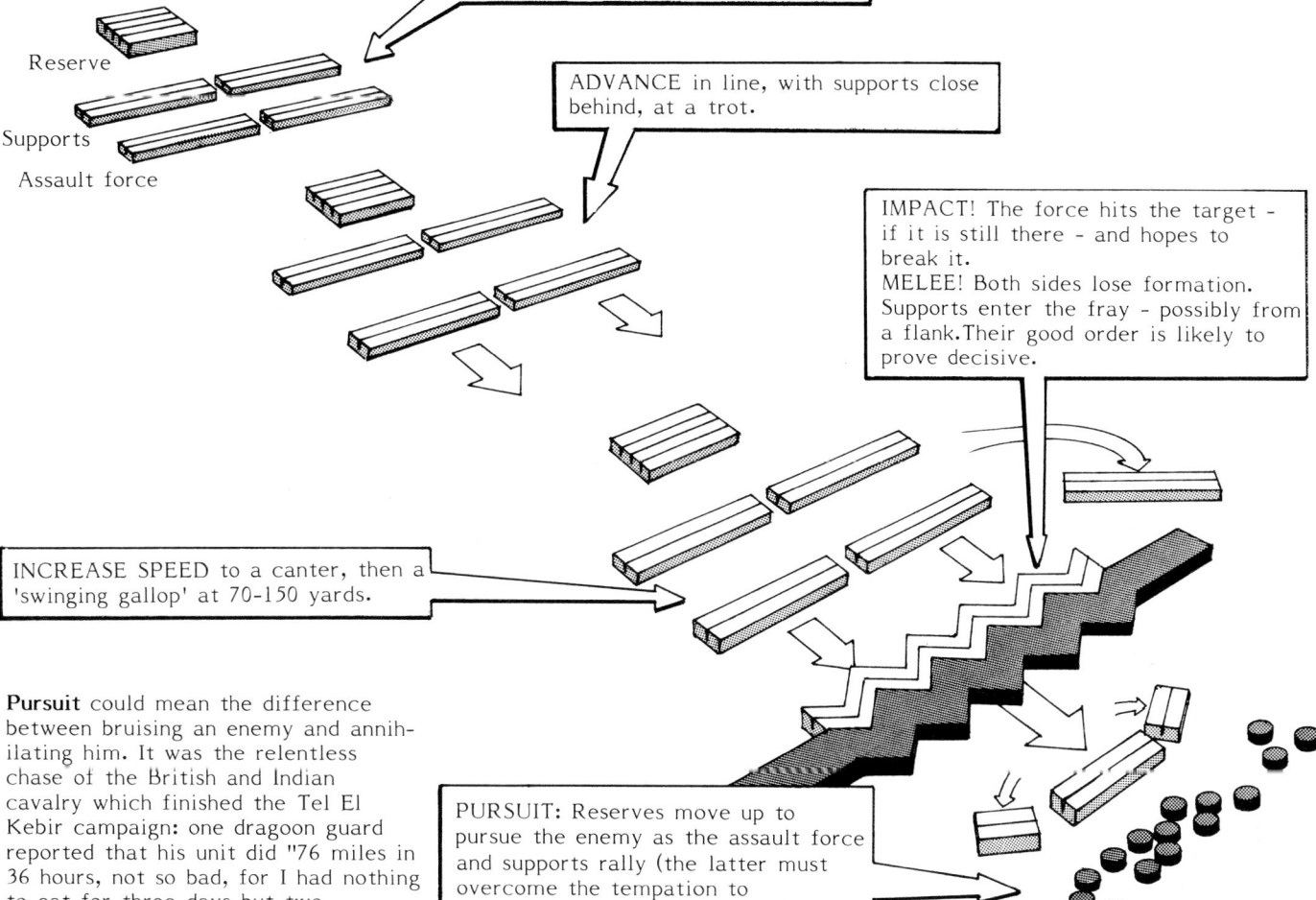

PREPARATION: leave fodder bags, and split force into -
Assault force (33-100% of available troops)
Supports (0-66%, 60-500 yards in rear)
Reserves (0-33%, 60 yards to several miles in rear)

Reserve
Supports
Assault force

ADVANCE in line, with supports close behind, at a trot.

IMPACT! The force hits the target - if it is still there - and hopes to break it.
MELEE! Both sides lose formation. Supports enter the fray - possibly from a flank. Their good order is likely to prove decisive.

INCREASE SPEED to a canter, then a 'swinging gallop' at 70-150 yards.

PURSUIT: Reserves move up to pursue the enemy as the assault force and supports rally (the latter must overcome the temptation to continue charging in confusion).

Pursuit could mean the difference between bruising an enemy and annihilating him. It was the relentless chase of the British and Indian cavalry which finished the Tel El Kebir campaign: one dragoon guard reported that his unit did "76 miles in 36 hours, not so bad, for I had nothing to eat for three days but two biscuits..." Foot pursuit could be equally effective. The fleet-footed Zulus destroyed the remains of the Isandhlwana garrison as they fled back over the Buffalo River, while the marching prowess of the Italian Askaris converted the drawn battle of Coatit into a triumph. On the other hand, many victories were never adequately exploited. The end of combat was usually a time of exhaustion for a commander and his troops, and Europeans could not in any case hope to catch a departing African. The Boers especially wasted many opportunities for pursuit - partly from fatigue, but partly from their own distinctive character. When Piet Joubert was implored to pursue after the battle of Ladysmith (1899) he replied 'When God holds out a finger, don't take the whole hand'.

Retreat from a lost battle was one of the most difficult tasks that might confront a commander. Few African armies had effective plans for such a contingency, and the Zulus placed such a total emphasis on the need for victory that their morale broke completely if they were defeated, so they would offer little resistance to pursuers. In contrast to this, the Mahdists beaten at Abu Klea (1885) remained unbowed, and simply walked away from the field.

Most defeated armies tried to get away as fast as possible. Deneys Reitz said of the Boer retreat from Natal, "No march order was given; we were simply told to go and it was left to each man to carry out his own retirement". European regulars were - at least in theory - trained to withdraw systematically from difficult situations. A rearguard would be formed of steady troops. In irregular warfare they would stay close to the main body to avoid encirclement. Under the guidance of officers, the troops would fall back and rally at a chosen position. Accounts of the Italian rearguard after Adowa point to the heroic efforts of Baratieri and his officers to create knots of formed men to stave off pursuit. If morale failed, however, there was little the commander could do to stop the rout: in the actions around Dundee and Ladysmith (1899) the British retreats seemed to collapse into anarchy for no apparent reason.

37

Horrible Disasters

The possibility of disaster dogged every action taken by any European commander. One error, one failure to perceive what was going on, could mean the destruction of his command, blazing headlines in the papers and angry questions in the government - things to be feared far more than death itself. Disasters demanded explanations, scapegoats, revenge. In 1904 the Portuguese sent 2,000 men to avenge the loss of 300 at Cuamoto in Angola. The British and Germans sent many more to recover their prestige after embarrassments in Southern Africa (great caution was needed to prevent the Queen receiving bad news at the breakfast table!). Yet catastrophe did sometimes strike: forces were surprised, or blundered into trouble, or got lost. Supplies ran out, camps were overrun, units broke and fled. In this section we look at a few examples of what 'Horrible disaster' might mean.

El Eilafun (September 1884) was an Egyptian defeat caused by overconfidence. General Gordon's best subordinate, Mohammed Pasha, had made a series of successful sorties to disperse the Mahdist forces surrounding Khartoum. After a victory at Halfaya 'the Fighting Pasha' decided on a foray up the Blue Nile to smash an enemy concentration by the Sheikh-El-Obeid. He won a sharp action, resupplied, and then - leaving a force entrenched on the right bank - chased the Mahdists into heavy thorn bush. Separated from the firepower of his gunboat support, Mohammed was surrounded, overwhelmed and died with sword in hand. El Eilafun was a debacle for Gordon's defence of Khartoum: he lost 800 of his best troops, 980 Remington rifles and his most capable commander.

Lugalo (August 1891), in the Tanganyika region, was a German defeat attributable to poor march security. Commander Emil von Zelewski, known as 'the hammer', was advancing towards a rocky hill amidst thick grass. He had three companies of the 'Defence Force' - some 260 men - with three artillery pieces and a baggage train. At about 7am on the 17th the main body was assaulted by 3,000 Hehe warriors who had crept unseen to within 30 yards. Zelewski was killed and his column overwhelmed. The rearguard commander, Tettenborn, managed to rally the remnants on a knoll and held off the enemy through the day and into the night. The Hehe had a few firearms and relied on Zulu-style tactics learned from Ngoni groups from the south. At dawn on the 18th they set fire to the grass to cover their withdrawal, taking with them three guns, 300 rifles and most of the stores. German casualties were 10 officers and ncos, 200 Askaris and 96 porters. Only four Europeans and 60 Askaris survived.

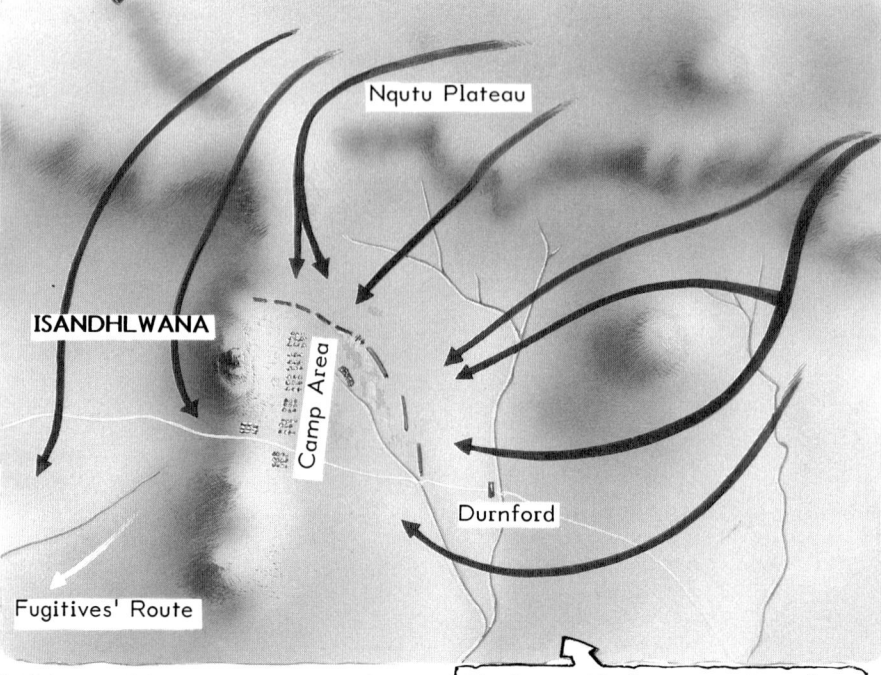

Isandhlwana (January 1879) is probably the best-known European disaster in Africa. Lord Chelmsford, in search of the Zulus' main Impi, had split his forces into several columns. The Vanguard of one column had found a group of enemy, so he went to join it. This left the forward supply base at Isandhlwana garrisoned by six companies - 597 men - of the 24th Foot, two guns, 115 mounted troops and 431 of the Natal Native Contingent. The camp was not fortified, despite advice, and there was a confusion of command responsibility between Lt Col Pulleine of the 24th and the newly-arrived Col Durnford. Zulu forces were spotted on the plateau above the camp and on the plain ahead. Pulleine deployed his companies in an extended line a mile from his tents, while Durnford took his Basuto horsemen on ahead. This thin defence was assailed by 20,000 Zulus, who at first were held in check by the British fire. But then Durnford's men ran short of ammunition and were forced to retire. The Zulus rushed forward as Pulleine moved up a company to cover them. The Natal Natives broke and the regulars were overwhelmed. Durnford fell in a last stand and the drifts of the Buffalo river became clogged with fugitives. Of 950 Europeans only 55 survived, while most of the Natal Contingent was also killed. 2,000 Zulus fell - a grievous loss; "An assegai has been thrust into the belly of the nation", said Cetshwayo.

The heavy black arrows show the development of the classic Zulu concentric attack. The enemy was engaged frontally while the 'Horns' rapidly enveloped the flanks of his position.

Battle in Africa

Adowa (March 1st 1896) was an overwhelming Italian disaster which arose out of the combination of several lesser mistakes, none of which was necessarily catastrophic in itself. Baratieri, governor of Eritrea, had an army of 56 guns and 17,700 men, including 10,596 Italians. Provisions were short and many of the new arrivals from Italy were green - but morale was high. The Ethiopian army was known to be on the verge of retreat through hunger and Baratieri had been honour bound, by Prime Minister Crispi, to press forward. After a council with his brigadiers, he decided on a night march to a mountain position overlooking Menelik's camp. The Ethiopians would then be forced either to attack or withdraw ignominiously.

Things went wrong from the start. Baratieri and his senior Brigadier, Arimondi, mistrusted each other. 1,200 native troops were absent due to a telegraphic error. Worst of all, the maps confused the hill designated as the left of the chosen line with another four miles out of position. Thus when General Albertone reached the correct place after a moonlit march of six hours, his guides assured him he still had further to go. Since he had arrived before Arimondi's centre brigade was in sight, Albertone believed he was wrong and continued the march. At 5.45 his vanguard ran into a huge body of Ethiopians and battle was joined. The Italians held their ground for several hours, but then the left flank battalion was overrun by some 15,000 enemy. The rest of the brigade began to retire and was then completely destroyed.

On the extreme right General Dabormida tried to link up with Albertone, but his line of march via the mountain passes led him further away, and into a hornets' nest of Shoan warriors. This left Baratieri's selected flank positions unoccupied, and they were seized by Abyssinians pursuing fugitives from Albertone's force. From here Arimondi was taken in flank, then Baratieri's reserve brigade was overrun during an attempted deployment. Each one of the three remaining commands was isolated and overwhelmed. Arimondi and Dabormida both died fighting, and their men finally lost their discipline in a general 'sauve-qui-peut' about noon. The Shoans pursued for about nine miles, capturing some 4,000 men. Altogether 43% of the Italians were killed, wounded or missing.

Abyssinian movements ⬛➡   **Italian movements** ⬜➡

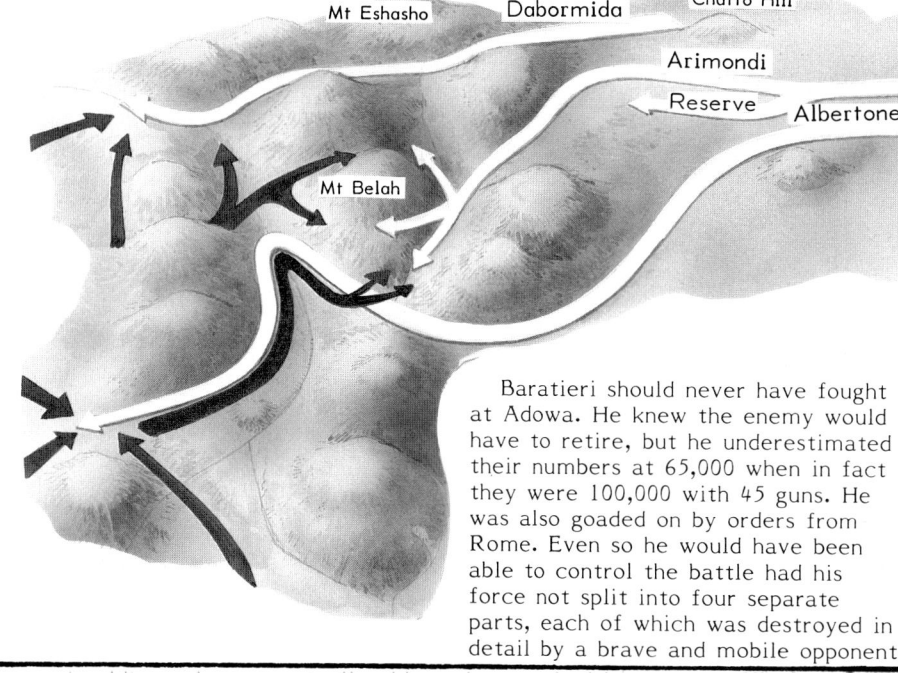

Baratieri should never have fought at Adowa. He knew the enemy would have to retire, but he underestimated their numbers at 65,000 when in fact they were 100,000 with 45 guns. He was also goaded on by orders from Rome. Even so he would have been able to control the battle had his force not split into four separate parts, each of which was destroyed in detail by a brave and mobile opponent.

Stormberg Junction (December 1899) was an astonishing example of how a difficult operation - a night attack - could turn into a complete fiasco. Lt Col Gatacre planned to attack Boer positions on the heights above Stormberg and seize the railway junction. He intended to move 2,700 men to Molteno by rail on 9th December, then cover the ten miles to Stormberg on foot overnight and make a frontal assault at dawn. This was changed to a flank attack - adding several miles to the march - after erroneous information was received that the Boer position was strengthened by wire. The execution proved disastrous; after lengthy delays Gatacre left Molteno with only part of his force, and got lost. After hours of marching through rocky terrain arguing with his guides, he eventually reached the enemy outposts. Unfortunately he believed them to be six miles distant, so he blundered into them unexpectedly. The infantry charged up a steep crag, were shelled by their own guns and fell back. An irate farmer started firing at soldiers who were stealing his sheep. Gatacre lost all control and ordered a retreat which turned into a scramble for home. Losses appeared light - 29 killed and 57 wounded - but when the troops assembled, several hundred were missing. They had not heard the recall and remained on the kopje above Stormberg, to be captured when morning came. The Boers, only 800 strong, rounded up 633 bemused officers and men forgotten in Gatacre's retreat.

The Flatters Expedition set out from Ouargla in Algeria (December 1880) to survey a projected stretch of the Trans-Sahara Railway. There were 11 Frenchmen and 77 Tirailleurs Algériens and Goumiers. Despite careful planning and a train of 300 camels, water became short almost 500 miles into the desert - eight days beyond the last well. Lt Col Flatters accepted an invitation from a Tuareg band to accompany them to the nearest wells and return with water. Taking the camels and 37 officers and men, he marched into a trap. His force was destroyed, apart from a few survivors who brought word to Lieut Dianous, commander of the remnant of the expedition. He ordered a retreat - on foot - to cover a distance that had taken 2½ months by camel. Dianous kept careful precautions against ambush, since a large group of Tuareg was reported shadowing the column. He had plenty of ammunition, if little else, and he may have hoped to provoke a fight. The Tuareg - apparently out of pity - gave the troops some dates, but they were poisoned. Some died and others were driven mad. As the column staggered to the first large well the Tuareg charged and were beaten off by volleys. After this they kept their distance, but Dianous was killed by a sniper. The men ate lizards, leather belts, camel bones, and then their own dead. The last Frenchman, a sergeant, was killed and eaten. Finally the thirsty, raving survivors reached a French post to tell their story, some eight weeks after Flatters had been killed.

Glorious Victories

'Glorious Victory!' What better to read about on the down train from Epsom or in a cafe by the Seine? It was these victories that kept taxpayers from grumbling and governments from crumbling. Victorian myth thrived on heroism - and in victory heroism was combined with glory, honour, and the chance of rapid promotion for the officers. In this section we look at some of the occasions on which the Europeans managed to use tactics almost 'according to the book'. Despite the difficulties, dangers and uncertainties, military forces could sometimes manage to achieve everything they were supposed to, and to co-ordinate a flank attack, or pre-plan a frontal assault, exactly according to the needs of the moment.

Bedden and Rejjaf The use of flanking movements is well illustrated by the victories of Congo Free State forces at Bedden and Rejjaf on 17th February 1897, on the upper Nile. Commandant Chaltin was encamped at Bedden with 700 infantry of the Force Publique, 580 Azande irregulars and a small Krupp gun. About 1,600 yards to the north, some 1,200 Mahdists were holding a 'strong position... a natural fort'. Advancing in column with the river to the right and the irregulars to the left, Chaltin halted at 400 yards and deployed five of his eight platoons in line, holding the remainder in reserve with the Azande. The Mahdists opened fire: the Congolese artillery replied, but the infantry did not. After 30 minutes, at 7.30 am Chaltin advanced another 200 yards. The Mahdists began an attack against his left flank, so he threw in two reserve platoons against them, and sent the Azande on a wide sweep around the enemy in a double envelopment. This broke the attackers away from their main body and forced them to flee. At the same time - 8 am - the three platoons on the Congolese right charged the ridge and cleared it with the bayonet in 20 minutes. The Mahdists fell back, having lost their Emir, Muhammad Ali Badi. Chaltin rested his men until 10.30, then followed the foe. At 1.30 the advance guard observed that the Mahdists had taken up another ridge position between Mount Rejjaf and the Nile. In a repeat of the morning action, Chaltin's men smashed the Mahdist line by a frontal assault while the Azande circled to the left and attacked the enemy rear. By 5.30 the Mahdist base on the upper Nile was in Free State hands, and they had lost perhaps 200 killed, as against Chaltin's loss of 100 killed and 160 wounded.

Member of the 'Force Publique'

Coatit (13th January 1895) shows a variant of the night march/dawn attack theme. General Baratieri had found Ras Mangasha's Tigrean army encamped in a valley, unaware of his presence. An early morning march placed the Italian force - three good battalions of Askaris (c 3,300 men), four mountain guns and 400 irregulars - into a position overlooking the Ethiopian camp. Baratieri's plan was not to storm the bivouac, but to hold the high ground and provoke an enemy attack. Sure enough, the Tigreans charged frontally at the same time as they attempted to turn the Italian left. Mangasha himself led the flanking movement, forcing Baratieri to change his front and start a withdrawal. This was done skilfully: an Italian firing line was established and a prolonged fusillade began which continued all day, and on into the next. At 10 pm on the 14th Ras Mangasha and his 22,000 warriors withdrew. Baratieri did not pursue until the following day, when his advance guard caught up with the Tigreans. they were easily scattered, and a great haul of booty collected. Thus a drawn battle became a victory as a result of the regulars' better discipline and organisation.

Battle in Africa

Sidi Bou Othmann The offensive use of the square is well exemplified by the French victory at Sidi Bou Othmann on 6th September 1912. Col. Charles Mangin (later known as 'the butcher' at Verdun) had been ordered to march on Marrakesh when a pretender to the Moroccan throne, El Hiba, had taken over the city. Forming his 5,000 men into two squares - a 'fighting square' and a 'convoy square' for the 3,500 animals - Mangin came against El Hiba's 10-15,000 men, the core of them Saharan nomads. Both sides advanced. The Moroccans opened fire at 1,600 yards, wasting ammunition wildly, and began to envelop the square. At 8 - 900 yards the French opened up with Le Gras rifles, eight machine guns and twelves 75 mm QF cannon. The Moroccan crescent came on, masking the French from the fire of El Hiba's few ancient guns. The attack quickly collapsed and the Harka fled, leaving 2,000 dead on the plain. Mangin's loss was two dead and 23 wounded.

Tsynainondry was a French victory in September 1895, which showed how a campaign could be won less by fighting than by survival in extreme tropical conditions. Faced with more than 340 miles of Madagascar's swamp and jungle, and virulent diseases that killed 10% of his force in two months, General Duchesne decided to abandon his lines of communication, his 5,000 'Lefebvre chariots' (metal carts), and the bulk of his command. He chose 4,000 men, gave them 3,000 mules, twelve guns and food for three weeks, then led them towards Tananarive. Hacking through the rain forest, men dying by the side of the track, the force fell foul of the traditional Malagasy weapons of forest and fever. When it reached Tsynainondry, however, though weak from hunger, it was still able to fight. The Hova royal army, the Foloalindahy, was entrenched on a mountainside, but the Foreign Legion simply marched over it. The greatest opposition proved to be a herd of stampeding pigs which 'ran out of a village and attacked the legionnaires'.

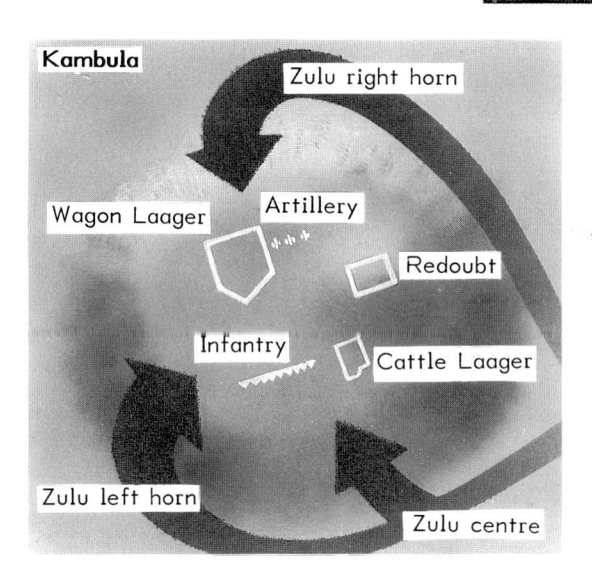

Buller's light horsemen pursue the fleeing Zulus after Kambula.

Kambula was a British victory on 29th March 1879, which shows how a defensive battle could be used as part of an offensive strategy. In order to bring on a general action on his own terms, Col. Sir Evelyn Wood had sent a strong force to attack the Zulus' herds on Hlobane, a mountain some 15 miles distant. The operation itself was disastrous, but its effect was to bring 24,000 Zulus to assault Wood's own chosen position. His command was small - 2,000 men and six 7 pdrs. - but his site was well selected and fortified. Three works - a laager, a cattle kraal and a redoubt - had been placed to give mutual support on a hilltop. As the Impi approached, Buller led a mounted force out to trigger a premature attack by its right 'horn'. This brought an immediate assault, which was broken up by massed fire. More threatening was the attack by the Zulu left and centre, which used the 'dead ground' of a ravine to get within 200 yards of the south face. A company holding the cattle kraal was forced to retire: Zulu riflemen took their position and covered the advance of their comrades. Wood ordered a bayonet charge, which threw back the enemy. Even using captured British Martini rifles, the Zulus were unable to make effective use of fire, and after four hours their attack slackened. A second sortie from the laager recaptured the kraal and lined the rim of the dead ground below. As the Zulus began to retreat, Buller led a relentless pursuit with his mounted volunteers, harrying the beaten Impi for several miles.

Guerrilla Warfare

For some African peoples guerrilla warfare was a natural recourse once full-scale war had failed. For others, however, it was the standard first response to any invasion by a strong intruder. The essential requirements were threefold:-
1 Mobility: the guerrilla needs greater effective mobility than his adversary, be it by horse, camel or fleetness of foot.
2 Intelligence: Information from civilians or scouts on enemy actions is essential, as is disinformation to the foe about one's own.
3 Logistic support: Guerrillas cannot live without access to food, clothing, weapons, ammunition, horses &c.

If these needs could be filled, quite small numbers of men, operating without firm bases, could wage effective campaigns of harassment against an occupying power. At El Moungar we have seen a Moroccan raid directed not at the enemy's outposts, but at his convoys. Similar approaches were used by the 'Mad Mullah' of Somalia - whose camels kept him beyond British reach until the advent of aircraft - by Samori, and by the Rhodesian peoples. At a lower level, 'social bandits' such as Mapondera - who fought both the British and the Portuguese (1892-1903) - committed crimes against such symbols of oppression as taxmen, labour recruiters or government warehouses.

The Hottentots of Namibia proved steadfast and successful adversaries to the Germans. More sophisticated in their understanding of the Europeans than most African peoples, they used traditional fieldcraft skills to outmanoeuvre and outwit their foes. With captured rifles, ammunition and horses, the bands of Hendrik, Cornelius and Morenga waged an effective guerrilla war between 1904 and 1907. Cornelius began in April 1905 with a series of lightning raids against German outposts, then outran pursuing columns and joined Morenga in the Karras hills. In March 1906, however, he surrendered, leaving 'the robber chieftain' Joseph Morenga alone in the field. Morenga was a skilled strategist who used scouts to inform him of German plans, so that he could avoid their converging columns. When he fought, it was from ambush: in one of a series of successful traps, he pinned four companies of the Field Force against the Orange River at Hartebeestmund (October 1905). Stationing his men on islands in the river and in the dunes beyond the north bank, Morenga laid down a crossfire that inflicted 43 German casualties at no cost to his own band.

Morenga's band of Hottentots, while they adopted European dress and weapons, lost none of their African fieldcraft skills.

Elsewhere he captured convoys, over-ran posts and stole horses until eventually forced to retire to Bechuanaland, where he was killed by Cape Police in 1908. With less than 400 riders he had tied up 13 mounted companies - at least 2,000 men with ten field- and eight machine guns - for a period of two years. At times he had been outnumbered by twenty to one.

Forest Peoples relied on guerrilla techniques far more than on large scale actions. Skirmishing from the bush, ambushing columns strung out along jungle trails, attacking files of porters or stragglers - these could be very effective methods. In 1891 the Baule of the Ivory Coast, led by Etien Komenan, defeated one French column and two years later forced a second to retreat. It was led by J B Marchand (of Fashoda fame), and he was able to prevail only when he returned with a third column in greater strength. In the Congo some 5,000 rubber workers rebelled against Leopold's exactions and maintained a fight from forest hideouts from 1899 to 1908. In Gambia in 1894 a Royal Navy landing party was ambushed on the beach by Fode Sila's war boys, losing 54 casualties out of 200 before the ships were regained. Such successes were usually followed by eventual defeat, but at least they represented the most effective use of terrain by forces with limited manpower.

Battle in Africa

The Boer Commandos channelled their efforts into guerrilla warfare from the middle of 1900 onwards. Independent commandos, loosely co-ordinated by such senior leaders as Botha, De La Rey, De Wet and Smuts, operated throughout the Free State and Transvaal, and even into the Cape. Rail lines were torn up, telegraphs cut, convoys seized, small posts overrun. Sustained by the charity of the Dutch population, and by what they could forage or capture, the Bitter-Enders fought on in the hope that 'something would turn up'. Between October 1900 and September 1901 they cut the railway on average 16 times a month, and in three months it was 30 times or more. Nevertheless by the winter of 1901 the commandos were in dire straits. Many horses died and the men were in rags, reduced to scouring British campsites for dropped cartridges. Yet morale remained high, and Boer victories at Bakenlaagte, Groenkop and Vlakfontein (1901) and Tweebosch (1902) kept the war alive. At war's end on 31st May 1902 there remained 18,000 tattered but unbowed burghers in the field. Indeed, Jan Smuts' commandos had even taken control of much of the isolated Western Cape region.

The European Response to guerrilla warfare could take several forms. In Madagascar Gallieni used a 'hearts and minds' policy, as did Lyautey in Morocco (although it was backed up, and often superseded, by repression and Razzia). In South Africa Lord Roberts began a policy of conciliation, but under Kitchener emphasis was placed on efforts to undermine the Boers' logistic base. Farms were burnt, livestock slaughtered, women and children rounded up into concentration camps: these harsh measures failed to break the Boer will to resist - rather the contrary - but they did slowly shut down their means of supply. To protect the vital railways a system of blockhouses was developed, which also served to prevent easy crossing of the tracks - thereby reducing the mobility of the commandos. At first independent columns were used - often several hundred horsemen with a few guns - but increasingly dependence was placed on large scale 'drives' to sweep large areas clear of enemy men, horses and cattle. These were expensive and seemed to produce small results - but were more effective than any other technique.

In SW Africa the Germans followed a policy of 'Schrecklichkeit' against the Hereros, killing thousands of women and children by forcing them into the Omaheke desert. Rewards were offered for rebel leaders; prisoners were shot; proclamations of dire intent were issued. These measures proved to be entirely counter-productive, however, until eventually a new system was developed under von Deimling. He instituted 'flying squads' to cover specific areas. Each Hottentot band would then be pursued by successive columns of fresh troops, forcing the exhausted raiders to fight or abandon their booty. This approach, combined with the removal of livestock out of the war zone, finally made the conflict too costly for the guerrillas.

'New Model Drive 1902'

The first of these involved 300 blockhouses, 7 armoured trains & 17,000 troops. It failed to catch De Wet but cost the Boers 286 killed, wounded and captured.

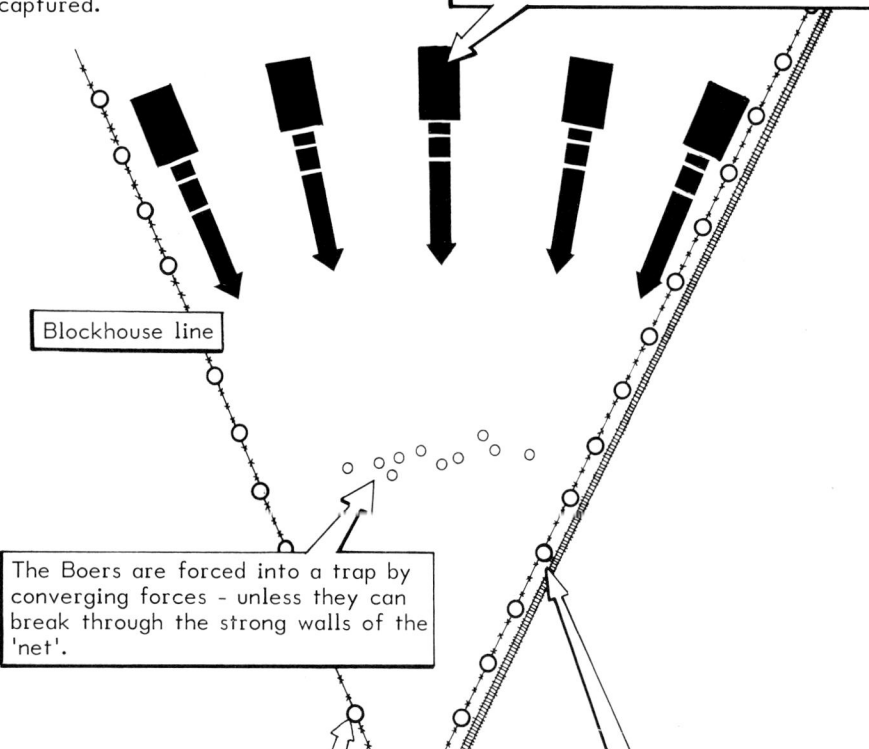

The 'driving columns' form up on a 60 mile frontage, narrowing as they drive into the angle created by the blockhouse and railway lines.

Blockhouse line

The Boers are forced into a trap by converging forces - unless they can break through the strong walls of the 'net'.

Railway line, protected by blockhouses and patrolled by armoured trains with searchlights.

By the end of the Boer war, over 8,000 blockhouses were garrisoned. This is an early production version of the prefabricated type, the later 'pepperpot' model had a circular roof. The Iron walls were double skinned, sandwiching a bullet-proof layer of shingle. Each fort slept six or seven. Originally placed some 2,500 yards apart, later lines of blockhouses were denser. All were connected by barbed wire entanglements.

Siege Warfare

Siege warfare as a distinct form of action was relatively rare in African conflicts. Fortresses were regarded as refuges rather than as strategic strongholds, and assaults upon them traditionally followed the usual rules of the battlefield, rather than more specialised engineering methods. Prolonged sieges were very much the product of the Europeans' arrival and the longest (Mafeking, 217 days) occurred during the 'White Man's' war in South Africa.

African Fortresses fell into three broad categories:-

1 Temporary Defence Works: some were rudimentary, others very elaborate. At their most basic, a simple enclosure to keep livestock in and predators out could be erected from branches and bushes in a short time. It could then be strengthened with more wood and thorn-bush; with a ditch, a firing step or a rifle trench. Mahmud's zariba on the bank of the Atbara River (1898) involved a series of ditches, stockades and rifle pits dug behind the outer ring of thorn scrub - but, alas, the position was by no means as strong as it was complex: it was carried in 40 minutes by a determined assault. In South Africa the Boers added wire entanglements - sometimes arranged to make noise if touched - to their entrenchments: at Paardeburg a laager of wagons was used to beat off Kitchener's assault and became the scene of a ten-day siege that eventually ended in the surrender of the starving garrison.

2 Permanent Fortifications: Islamic Africa was the home of stone and mud fortresses varying from small Moorish 'castles' to the walled cities of the Western Sudan. These presented an imposing appearance, and were effective against an enemy who possessed no artillery. Few were very strong against modern weaponry, however.

Also 'permanent', although requiring constant rebuilding, were the fortified towns of the Bantu peoples. Mirambo had a capital a half mile square with a population of 15,000 and a strong zareba of poisonous Euphorbia. It had supporting embankments and ditches, and a citadel built around the chief's quarters and armoury. When the kraal was stormed by Lt von Prince's German column in 1893, Mirambo's successor Siki blew himself up with the magazine after two days' fighting.

3 Natural Positions: These could be used as a defensive recourse. During the 1896 Ndebele and Shona rising, the rock formations of Taba Zi Ka Mambo and the Matopos provided valuable strongholds against Rhodes' columns. Throughout Southern Africa, too, settlements were often built on mountain sites - eg Sekukuni's 'Fighting Kop', 'Moorosi's Mountain' in Sotho territory and Makoni's kraal in Mashonaland. The more conventional fortifications of Northern Africa also gained from the strength of rugged terrain. The Ethiopian fortress at Magdala, which fell to Napier's 1868 expedition, was built on an inaccessible crag. Moroccan forts, such as Taghit in 1903 or the Rif villages, relied on commanding all approaches.

The Boer State-Artillery load the 6" Creusot gun 'Creechy' during the bombardment of Mafeking. Inset is a typical shelter or 'bombproof' occupied by the inhabitants of towns under fire during the Boer War.

European Siegecraft Most of the scientific theories of siege warfare, developed over centuries in Europe, were set aside in Africa. Few fortresses needed complex methods to attack: Oyo was captured in one day after a 12 pdr was brought up (1895), while Kitchener's gunboats and 60 lb Lyddite shells caused serious destruction to Omdurman the day before the great battle (1898). It was generally considered best to attack a position as soon as possible, overwhelming the defence and 'providing a demonstration' of European strength and moral fortitude. The attack on Sekukuni's stronghold (December 1879) shows something of a storming: "At 11.30 a rocket went up and the troops rushed forward on our side. The sappers were in the thick of it, and strange to say as we doubled over the open, though the bullets came very close, no one fell, and the men were soon swarming up the rocks like bees. It is impossible to describe things as they were then, shots coming out of holes all around which killed two or three poor fellows...the men fired down the holes and used their bayonets freely". The bayonet and clubbed rifle were the usual weapons in an assault, but in this incident our writer - an Engineer officer - used gun-cotton to blow up the Pedi caves ("not very glorious work"), and two decades later dynamite was used to defeat the Shona rebels in their rock retreats.

Battle in Africa

The Europeans Besieged As a siege approached, the commander of a garrison had a number of issues to address. If he resolved them effectively he would prolong resistance, and probably ensure success:-

1 Preparation of the Position: Earthworks would be dug, thorn or wire entanglements laid, buildings converted to hospitals, HQs & strongpoints. Gordon made improvised landmines at Khartoum, while at Kimberley a civilian engineer designed and built a 4.1" gun - 'Long Cecil' - in 24 days.

2 Organisation of the Defence: Arrangements for reserves and dividing the works into sectors of responsibility; civilians placed under military orders and told off as guards and workmen. Dealing with civilians posed special headaches: at Kimberley the garrison commander was effectively subordinated to Cecil Rhodes: at Khartoum Gordon was faced with a populace that showed strong signs of favouring the enemy.

3 Provision of Food and Water: This was a vital priority. At Macalle the Italians lost control of the water supply, and for 11 days the garrison lived on half a litre per day. At Khartoum the problem was food: in the final days the bread had to be made of palm fibre, and it made the men sick. A garrison commander would usually seek to take control of food supply to ensure fair distribution - although at Kimberley the African inhabitants starved while the prosperous whites had champagne and caviar in stock.

4 Provision for the Health of Garrison and Civilians: Disease was the inevitable consequence of siege. Within Ladysmith (1899-1900) there were 10,673 hospital admissions out of the 13,497-man garrison in a siege of 118 days: deaths from enteric fever were six times the losses from enemy action.

5 Maintenance of Morale and Military Effectiveness: A vigorous defence sorties against the enemy, 'high profile' leadership and continuing activity could all help a great deal. During the Boer War sieges the British commanders even resorted to concerts, sports and emergency newspapers in order to stave off idleness - making Robert Baden-Powell a national hero in the process.

African Siegecraft was rudimentary, and more often than not a well-supplied defender could expect simply to sit out his investment until the besieging army dispersed with its plunder. The options open to the besieging commander were limited:-

1 Simple Blockade: The attempt to starve out the defender was a low-risk choice, but it required an encircling force that was content to sit in enforced idleness for days, weeks or months. Most of the Boer sieges lapsed into a loose and lazy blockade. Deneys Reitz recalled the picnic-like atmosphere of the Transvaal lines around Ladysmith, with much hunting, visiting friends and swapping pleasantries with the enemy. This was probably the best that could be expected, since ill fortune, lack of provisions or the desire to go home could easily cause the dissolution of an army if its leaders were unable to keep motivation at a peak.

2 Bombardment: This would be aimed less at deliberate breaching of walls than at the discomfiture of the garrison and civilian population. At Kimberley the Boers used 6" Creusot 'Long Toms', causing much alarm albeit few casualties - 8,500 shells killed only 21 citizens. At Mafeking Baden-Powell sent the message "All well. Four hours' bombardment. One dog killed". Artillery was a rarity in African armies, however - eg the gift of a 75 mm cannon made the Moroccan Caid Madani El Glaoui a master of siegecraft and a Most Important Man (1893). Sporadic rifle fire was the best that most besieging armies could oppose to the defence. Although plunging fire inflicted heavy casualties on the Turcos holding a section of the ramparts at Fez in 1912, little more than desultory sniping was far more often the order of the day.

3 Assault: Always expensive, but potentially decisive. At El Obeid (1883) the Mahdi's attack failed disastrously with thousands killed: as a result of this experience he was unwilling to risk a storm of the Khartoum defences until in January 1885 it was a question of 'assault or retire'. At Macalle (1896) the Ethiopian assault was repulsed, so the blockade was resumed; while at Fez (1912) the failure of the assault brought demoralisation and dissolution for the Moroccan Harka. Success, however, would bring results both immediately - loot, slaves &c - and in the longer term, as waverers threw in their lot with the victors.

Followers of the Mahdi storm Gordon's defences at Khartoum.

After the Battle

In the aftermath of battle the sequence of events was as follows:

1 Rally and reform the victorious soldiery. If this was not done quickly, disaster could result. Outside Khenifra in 1914 a successful French dawn attack on a Moroccan camp degenerated into a Razzia of individual plundering. The enemy rallied, counter-attacked and wiped out 700 men, capturing ten machine guns and eight cannon.

2 Feed and - especially - water the men and animals.

3 Scour the battlefield - by moonlight if necessary - to recover the dead and wounded. In the Boer War a truce might be arranged for this purpose. Get the wounded to a dressing station, give the dead as much of a 'ceremonial' burial as the situation permits, and attend to enemy casualties in whatever manner seems appropriate. Hunt for items worth scavenging - souvenirs for the Europeans (eg Count Gleichen found a 'Birmingham billhook' on the field of Abu Klea); weapons and clothing for the Africans.

4 Write home to your family to confirm your survival, and to the families of fallen friends to inform them of their loss. The commander writes despatches for his superiors, while correspondents race to get their reports home first.

5 Collect the prisoners - if any - and make provision for them.

6 Handle any disciplinary duties, appoint officers to take the positions of those fallen, and carry on.

Victorious African Armies behaved differently from regular armies in several important respects. Restoring discipline after success was more difficult, as warriors sought plunder, slaves and livestock; and keeping the army together was a serious problem as men demanded to go home - particularly if they had not eaten in recent days. The Zulus and other Bantu peoples had certain prescribed rituals after combat: a warrior who had killed was obliged to rip open his victim's belly to release the spirit and to don the apparel of the slain. It was for this reason that after Isandhlwana Commandant Lonsdale failed to notice that the men in red coats were not Welshmen at all! A Zulu who had killed also had to follow cleansing ceremonies separated from his companions, which meant that the army melted away after Isandhlwana, and in defeat it might be too ashamed to return to the king at all! Other peoples had their own rituals after combat: in 1892 a young Belgian officer observed a cannibal ally cooking the leg of a slain enemy; "I knew it was horrible, but still, for the moment, we had to pretend not to see it..."

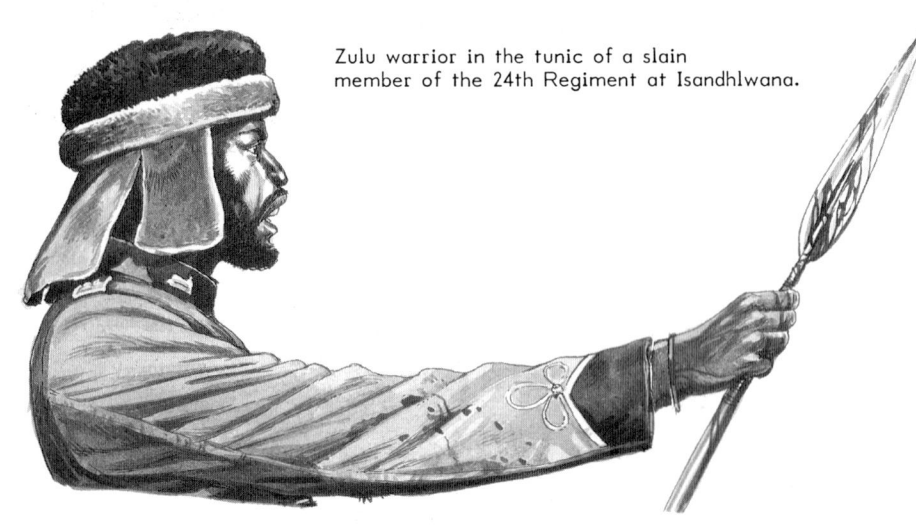

Zulu warrior in the tunic of a slain member of the 24th Regiment at Isandhlwana.

Prisoners Surrender was sometimes an option for men facing defeat. During the Boer Wars both sides were willing to give up when things got tough and - despite some alleged abuses of the white flag, and of misconduct towards prisoners during the last stages of the war- both sides treated most captives generously. At Bronkhorstspruit (1880) Boer civilians were highly attentive to British wounded who had been their enemies a few minutes earlier. By contrast, we have seen how injured Mahdists were killed by British and Egyptian troops, partly from fear they would turn on their would-be benefactors. In the disastrous 1889 Mahdist campaign Babikr Bedri recounts how he and his comrades chose to be 'captured' (they really 'deserted') once it was known that the Egyptians would accept their surrender.

The Zulus took no prisoners in battle, and were given no quarter in return. Even if a man succeeded in giving himself up, he was not necessarily safe. Herero prisoners handed over to the Germans by Hottentot scouts were summarily killed. Italians captured by the Ethiopians were often mutilated later, while torture - especially by women - was widely feared by soldiers. 'The last bullet' seemed a preferable choice. Even when treatment was good, the loss of freedom and exile from the homeland (eg Boer POWs sent to Bermuda or Ceylon, Samori Toure to Gabon), was not a prospect to relish. Good fortune could occur, however: Britons captured by Boers were sometimes disarmed - and even undressed! - then set free. Black soldiers of the Egyptian army were pressed into Mahdist service as 'Jehadia'.

What Were the Consequences of these 'Small Wars', these campaigns of imperial conquest? For Africans they spelt subjection to an alien authority which was sometimes distant, sometimes very clearly in evidence. Some peoples fared better than others, but the loss of independence applied to all. Whatever benefits the Europeans brought, it was clear that they had acquired African land and labour for their own purposes, and had deprived Africans of any say in matters of significance. These wars, in short, brought decades of subjection.

For the Europeans, and especially the soldiers, these wars brought adventure, sport and glory. For some they brought promotion and experience that was to bear fruit in the First World War: Kitchener, French, Haig, Gallieni and Joffre had all learned their trade in Africa. Some of the specific African lessons were also useful - eg the improvement in British fieldcraft in the years before 1914 was a result of the Boer War. Other lessons were less useful - eg in 1914 many believed the 'African' finding that cavalry had an excellent future in Europe. They missed the true lesson, that was adopted best by the German Lettow-Vorbeck between 1914 and 1918, which was that there were no strict rules; that 'the book' could be thrown away; that every situation had to be dealt with on its own terms.

Battle in Africa

The Wounded faced a serious ordeal, despite radical improvements in the standards of treatment since the Crimean and American Civil Wars. General anaesthesia now made operations less grim, but the care of casualties remained a difficult, painful business. The wounded were sorted out by 'triage' for attention immediately, later or - for some - never. Abdominal wounds, for instance, almost inevitably proved fatal and condemned the recipient to the third category.

A central principle of surgery was the massive 'debridement' of dead tissue around a wound - a brutal process aimed at the prevention of gas gangrene. Likewise limb wounds were likely to need amputation to avoid infection, and the treatment of shock was primitive. Until the major blood groups were identified in 1902 there were no transfusions, so saline solutions and strychnine were all that a physician could offer. The vast distances involved in African campaigns meant that particular attention was given to immediate treatment and safe transportation of casualties, rather than to the processing of large numbers of them. From 1884 German troops carried basic dressing kits, and by the Boer War the British were doing the same. Prompt treatment at Field Dressing Stations saved many lives, and provision for moving patients could be inventive - camel borne litters, hammocks carried by porters (but seldom comfortable), and so forth. Hospitals were often much worse - disease-ridden places where poor food, lack of basic supplies and neglect by third rate orderlies and doctors permitted infection to reach epidemic levels. Even the mixed blessings of modern medicine were denied to the Europeans' opponents: The Boers had a number of foreign volunteer ambulances (rejected by some in favour of herbal remedies) - but most Africans relied on traditional cures and religious or magical healing... often surprisingly successful, although the Zulus killed those of their wounded who obviously could not be helped.

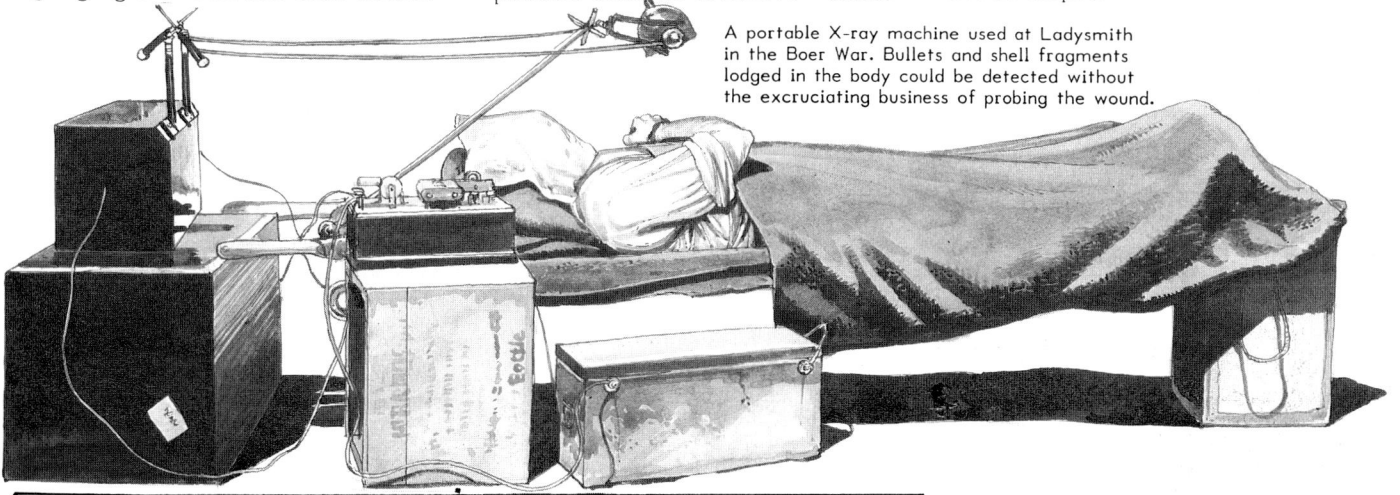

A portable X-ray machine used at Ladysmith in the Boer War. Bullets and shell fragments lodged in the body could be detected without the excruciating business of probing the wound.

Casualties in the unequal 'Maxim gun versus Spear' actions so common in Africa, the losses were often grossly unbalanced. At Coolela in Mozambique (1896) Galhardo's column defeated Gungunhama's 6-10,000 men within 40 minutes. 1,000 Portuguese troops inflicted heavy loss on their enemies but themselves lost only five dead. However when the Africans closed hand-to-hand, and especially if they won, the Europeans could take very heavy losses, as is shown by a survey of the Zulu War battles. Note that the Zulus averaged about 10% loss irrespective of whether they were victorious or defeated:-

Battle	British Present	British Loss	Zulus Present	Zulu Loss
Intombi Drift	106	78(75%)	800	80(10%)
Isandhlwana	1,774	1,329(73.5%)	c20,000	2,200(11%)
Hlobane	1,200*	202(25%)	2,000	?
Rorke's Drift	139	25(18%)	4,000	500(12.5%)
Kambula	1,998	83(4%)	24,000	2,200(9%)
Ulundi	5,124	113(2.2%)	18,000	1,200(6.5%)
Gingindhlovu	5,670	71(1.2%)	11,000	1,200(11%)
Inyezane	2,782	26(1%)	5,000	350(7%)

*includes 800 Swazi irregulars deserted during the action

In contrast the different style of warfare of the Boer War yields rather different figures. Casualties were almost all from shells or bullets and - except at Elandslaagte - the winners did not pursue. Aside from bloodbaths such as Spion Kop, where more than 50% of the British troops became casualties, losses were relatively light. Surprisingly, British casualties in the victories of Talana (11%) and Elandslaagte (8.7%) were higher than in the defeats of Colenso (6.2%) and Magersfontein (7%) - though individual battalions could suffer disproportionately heavily. On the Boer side, losses at Colenso were tiny (0.42%) but huge at Elandslaagte (27.7%). Other actions show a 3-7% loss, lower both in numbers and in proportion to their adversaries.

Sending the News Home was a feverish activity, as newsmen raced to get a 'scoop' and beat their rivals to the presses. After Ulundi Archibald Forbes rode alone across still-hostile country 300 miles in 50 hours to send his despatch. The telegraph could transmit the message rapidly, bringing joy or sorrow to the European public. The news of the relief of Mafeking was known in London on 18th May 1900, leading to exuberant 'Mafeking night' celebrations that were remembered by a whole generation.

Further Reading

The literature covering these African campaigns is extremely patchy. The larger British 'Small Wars' are very well covered, with a wide variety of Victorian accounts and more recent books. The French colonial wars have also produced a large body of work, although little of it is available in English translation. Likewise, there is much material in Italian on the wars of Menelik, but no recent English volume. The German, Belgian and Portuguese campaigns are very sparsely covered indeed. What follows is a list of useful 'starting points' for the reader.

GENERAL

A Adu Boahen "Africa Under Colonial Domination 1880 - 1935" (UNESCO 'General History of Africa', London 1985, Vol VII) Thorough work, very strong on the African viewpoint; Basil Davidson "Africa in Modern History" (London 1978); W L Langer "The Diplomacy of Imperialism" (New York, 1956); R Oliver & A Atmore "Africa since 1800" (Cambridge, 1972); R Robinson & J Gallagher "Africa and the Victorians" (London 1961).

MILITARY

Lawrence James "The Savage Wars - British campaigns in Africa 1870-1920" (London, 1985) Excellent recent study, strong on soldiers' experience and daily life; Frank Emery "Marching Over Africa" (London, 1986) Soldiers' letters from the Abyssinian war to the outbreak of the 2nd Boer War; Byron Farwell "Queen Victoria's little Wars" (New York, 1972) Concise, entertaining survey of British campaigns; C E Callwell "Small Wars, Their Principles and Practice" (London, 1896) The classic work on 'how to conduct a colonial war'; Hugh McLeave "The Damned Die Hard" (New York,1973) Colourful anecdotes of the French Foreign Legion - perhaps the best of a very mixed bunch on this subject.

THE ZULU WAR

Donald Morris "The Washing of the Spears" (New York, 1962) A classic account, but look also at the work of J J Guy and Sonia Clarke for recent revisions; Frank Emery "The Red Soldier" (London, 1977) A Marvellous collection of letters home from Zululand.

THE BOER WARS

O Ransford "The Battle of Majuba Hill" (London,1967); Thomas Pakenham "The Boer War" (London,1979); Byron Farwell "The Great Anglo-Boer War"(New York 1976); Deneys Reitz "Commando" (Johannesburg, 1929) A superb Boer Memoir.

THE HERERO/HOTTENTOT WARS

Jon Bridgeman "The revolt of the Hereros" (Berkeley 1981) H Bley "South West Africa under German Rule 1894-1914 (London, 1971).

WEST AFRICA

Michael Crowder "West African Resistance" (London 1971) An excellent source; and his "West Africa under Colonial Rule" (London, 1968); Frederick Myatt "The Golden Stool" (London 1966) On Asante 1900; A S Kanya-Forster "The Conquest of the Western Sudan" (London, 1970).

MOROCCO

Douglas Porch "The Conquest of Morocco" (London, 1982).

ETHIOPIA

G F Berkeley "The Campaign of Adowa and the rise of Menelik" (London, 1902).

RHODESIA/ZIMBABWE

T O Ranger "Revolt in Southern Rhodesia 1896-7" (London, 1967); F C Selous "Sunshine and storm in Rhodesia" (London 1896).

PORTUGUESE AFRICA

James Duffy "Portuguese Africa" (Harvard, 1961); Eric Axelson "Portugal and the Scramble for Africa 1875-91" (New York, 19--).

BELGIAN AFRICA

Ruth Slade "King Leopold's Congo" (London, 1962); R O Collins "The Southern Sudan" (Yale, 1962).

EAST AFRICA

D A Low, R Oliver et al "The Oxford History of East Africa" (2 vols, Oxford, 1962); Richard Meinertzhagen "Kenya Diary 1902-6" (London, 1959); John Iliffe "Tanganyika under German Rule" (Cambridge, 1969); Charles Miller "The Lunatic Express" (New York, 1972).

EGYPT/SUDAN

C Royle "The Egyptian Campaigns 1882-99" (London, 1900); W S Churchill "The River War" (London, 1899); Henry Kuen-Boyd "A Good Dusting" (London 1986); I H Zulfo "Karari, a Sudanese Account of Omdurman" (London, 1980); Babikr Bedri "Memoirs of a Mahdist" (Oxford, 1969).

PERIODICALS

"The Journal of African History" is the most important academic journal for the topic. "Soldiers of the Queen" is the excellent publication of the Victorian Military Society. "Savage and Soldier" is a wargames-oriented magazine devoted to the colonial wars of the 19th century.

WARGAME RULES

Larry Brom "The Sword and the Flame" is a fast-paced game of 'small wars' with a tongue-in-cheek feel; M Blake and I Colwill "The Colonial Skirmish Rules" gives a fairly detailed approach to man-to-man combat; Howard Whitehouse "Science versus Pluck, or too much for the Mahdi" provides historical roleplay and large scale actions in the Sudan campaigns.